'I wish this book had been available when I was beginning to learn about therapy. Mann, writing in his conversational style, draws the reader into gentle conversation with a wise elder who makes gestalt therapy accessible without reducing its wisdom.' – Lynne Jacobs, Ph.D., Co-Founder, Pacific Gestalt Institute, Los Angeles, CA, USA.

'I recommend this book to all practitioners, students and professionals, as well as to clients wishing to review the journey they have made with their therapist.' – Terry Browning, Gestalt Counsellor, London & Member of the British Association for Counselling and Psychotherapy.

'Whether you are familiar with Gestalt Therapy, or just starting out, this book is a must.' – Dr Sally Denham-Vaughan, UKCP Registered Gestalt Psychotherapist, Trainer, Supervisor and Writer.

Gestalt therapy offers a present-focused, relational approach, central to which is the fundamental belief that the client knows the best way of adjusting to their situation. By working to heighten awareness through dialogue and creative experimentation, gestalt therapists create the conditions for a client's personal journey to health.

Gestalt Therapy: 100 Key Points & Techniques provides a concise guide to this flexible and far-reaching approach. Topics discussed include:

- the theoretical assumptions underpinning gestalt therapy
- gestalt assessment and process diagnosis
- field theory, phenomenology and dialogue
- ethics and values
- evaluation and research.

As such this book will be essential reading for gestalt trainees, as well as established therapists, counsellors and psychotherapists wanting to learn more about the gestalt approach.

Dave Mann is a UKCP Registered Gestalt Psychotherapist, Supervisor and Trainer affiliated with the Metanoia Institute, Gestalt Psychotherapy Training Institute and Sherwood Psychotherapy Training Institute. He is also a former Assistant Editor of the British Gestalt Journal.

100 Key Points

Series Editor: Windy Dryden

ALSO IN THIS SERIES:

Cognitive Therapy: 100 Key Points and Techniques
Michael Neenan and Windy Dryden

Rational Emotive Behaviour Therapy: 100 Key Points and Techniques
Windy Dryden and Michael Neenan

Family Therapy: 100 Key Points and Techniques
Mark Rivett and Eddy Street

Transactional Analysis: 100 Key Points and Techniques
Mark Widdowson

Person-Centred Therapy: 100 Key Points and Techniques
Paul Wilkins

Gestalt Therapy

100 Key Points and Techniques

Dave Mann

Routledge
Taylor & Francis Group

LONDON AND NEW YORK

First published 2010 by Routledge
27 Church Lane, Hove, East Sussex BN3 2FA

Simultaneously published in the USA and Canada
by Routledge
711 Third Avenue, New York NY 10017

Routledge is an imprint of the Taylor & Francis Group, an Informa business

Reprinted 2011 (twice)

Typeset in Times by
RefineCatch Limited, Bungay, Suffolk
Printed and bound in Great Britain by
TJ International, Padstow, Cornwall
Paperback cover design by Andrew Ward

This publication has been produced with paper manufactured to strict
environmental standards and with pulp derived from sustainable
forests.

British Library Cataloguing in Publication Data
A catalogue record for this book is available from the British Library

Library of Congress Cataloging-in-Publication Data
Mann, Dave, 1957–
  Gestalt therapy : 100 key points & techniques / Dave Mann. – 1st ed.
    p. cm.
  Includes bibliographical references.
  1. Gestalt therapy. I. Title
  RC489.G4M355 2010
  616.89′143—dc22   2010004663

ISBN: 978-0-415-55293-6 (hbk)
ISBN: 978-0-415-55294-3 (pbk)

Contents

Preface

Just as our perception of the world in the present does not spring from a void, neither did gestalt therapy suddenly appear from nowhere. Just as our way of being in the world has a deep multi-layered history that shapes the way in which we relate now, so too was gestalt therapy's theory and practice shaped by the past multi-layered field prior to its conception. That field contained a rich diversity, creatively synthesized when the founders of the approach first published *Gestalt Therapy* (Perls, Hefferline and Goodman, 1951 – hereafter referred to as 'PHG'). The process of creating a truly integrative approach from gestalt's rich ground is reflected in the personal journeys of its founders – Frederick 'Fritz' Perls, Laura Perls and Paul Goodman. They learnt experi-entially in an embodied way and this is mirrored in the founding text and throughout gestalt theory. This rich ground, which we can think of as fertile earth supporting the acorn's growth into an oak tree, contains amongst others such philosophies as: holism, existentialism, phenomenology, field theory, dialogue and Eastern philosophies such as Zen Buddhism and Taoism. All were part of the pre-existing fertile ground from which gestalt emerged and continues to form the ground upon which it stands today. The way in which these philosophies – which might at this point appear to be a confusing collection of terms – integrate to create gestalt therapy will unfold over the next 100 points.

Gestalt therapy is as much an art as it is a science. We need the science of theory, research and technique to support us in our work in the clinical setting where we lead with the art of the approach – intuition, creativity and immediacy. What art and therapy have in common is that both create something new from something that has existed in a different form. Practising gestalt therapy is like making art: the artist's flair is supported by the scientific knowledge needed to create the paint and learn the method. In creating something unique and meaningful, form is given to human experience.

My initial reaction when asked to write this book was to drop 'and techniques' from the title. This was in reaction to some mis-conceptions in the wider field about gestalt being all about tech-niques such as talking to 'the empty chair' or dramatic emotional catharsis (usually anger). Cobbling together a few expressive experiments might be fine for a drama group's warm-up exercise but it is not gestalt therapy. However, my change of heart was because we do use techniques in gestalt therapy, but we do not lead with them. The use of techniques emerges in the relationship to help facilitate awareness but the relationship comes first. In gestalt we believe that the person before us holds the wisdom to know what is needed in relation to their situation. In that sense techniques are used to surface what is already known.

As you read this book I will invite you to engage in experiential exercises designed to heighten your awareness of specific points being discussed. There are also several case descriptions and brief 'transcripts' from my practice to help illuminate points all of which, to preserve confidentiality, are referred to by pseudonyms and are composite pictures. In the interests of equality I have alternated the use of 'he', 'she' and the less immediate 'they' and alternated the gender of the therapist. As I see gestalt therapy to be about discovery you will note that I have structured *Gestalt Therapy: 100 Key Points & Techniques* as a journey. Gestalt experimentation is used at different phases of a therapeutic journey with a client, so to be consistent with the practice that process is paralleled within these pages. You can if you wish drop in on this journey at one particular point, but be mindful that you will be lacking some of the background of the journey so far should you elect to do so.

Due to restrictions in space and to assist flow I will use short-hand in many of my explanations. For instance, when I use the term 'figure' as in 'figure and ground' I use the term to mean 'the dynamic, ever-changing process between figure and ground'. It just gets a little word laden if I use such phrases on every occasion! I hope this does not lead to misunderstandings but as, 'in the beginning is relation' (Buber, 1958: 18) I invite the reader to view anything written through a relational lens. I apologize in advance if my individualistic culture blinds me to this fundamental gestalt principle on occasions.

It might have been an interesting experiment to ask 100 gestalt therapists to list what they would consider 100 key points and techniques in gestalt therapy. My guess is that I would have ended up with 100 different and diverse variations, but then that is gestalt. Every gestalt therapist will form his or her own therapeutic philosophy from the common ground of gestalt's rich theory shaped by their own personal journey; every individual will integrate that theory differently just as every human being patterns their experience in their own unique way. No two gestalt therapists will be the same but both will be recognizable as gestalt therapists. To return to my earlier analogy – when was the last time you saw two identical oak trees?

Acknowledgements

I was originally invited to contribute to this book by two close colleagues familiar with my unpublished work. For sound but different reasons those colleagues had to withdraw, so it was over to you, Dave! As a virgin author writing this book has been a challenge but I just couldn't resist it and have no regrets on embarking upon the project. Part of the cost though has been sacrificing a substantial amount of time with my family and friends. Above all I owe a deep debt of gratitude to my wife, Karin, whose consistent love and support in my background I can take for granted. I also extend my apologies to my grandchildren Ruari and Otto for being out of contact with them for large chunks of time.

I am fortunate to have many professional supports, too many to adequately acknowledge here. One who has generously given me more than she may be aware is my dear friend and colleague, Sally Denham-Vaughan. Such has been her influence over the years that some of her theoretical sharing will be embedded in this book. Another is Malcolm Parlett whose fine mind and humanity it has been my privilege to be touched by. Both Sally and Malcolm kindly offered free consultations in the formulation of this text. Whilst these meetings were undoubtedly helpful it was the supportive ground formed through such eminent gestalt therapists showing faith in me that confirmed my ability to complete this venture.

Further thanks are extended to my 'review team' – Lynne Brighouse, Kate Glenholmes, Breda Kenda and Shaheen Mitha, for their feedback on pitch and clarity during the early stages of constructing this work. A far from comprehensive list of trainers and colleagues who have helped shape my thinking through introjection, agreement and/or disagreement over the years in chronological order include: Ian Greenway, Ken Evans, Des Kennedy, Richard Erskine, Petruska Clarkson, Rich Hycner, Judith Hemming, Lynne Jacobs, Lynda Osborne, Phil Joyce, Gary Yontef, Sally Denham-Vaughan, Frank Staemmler, Malcolm Parlett, Gordon Wheeler and Peter Philippson.

Thanks also to Jay Gort for his help with illustrations, to the supportive editorial team at Routledge and of course to the many clients, supervisees and trainees it has been my privilege to meet.

During the course of writing this book my father died. Together with my mother's quiet presence, I am fortunate that their love, care and pride in their children's achievements lives on. I dedicate this book to my mother and in my father's memory.

Part 1

MAPS FOR A GESTALT THERAPY JOURNEY: THEORETICAL ASSUMPTIONS UNDERPINNING THE APPROACH

1

What is gestalt?

Gestalt is a German word, a noun that has no direct English equivalent with its closest translation generally agreed to be pattern, form, shape or configuration. Yet it is more than any of these descriptions. In German it relates to the overall appearance of a person, their totality, where their energy is located. As is inevitably the case with any translation something is lost in the translation, and these terms do not fully convey its meaning. They are as close as those of us without an understanding of the German language can get. Indeed, even if we had an intimate understanding of the language each of us would create a slightly different picture from the word; such is the nature of language. In that sense I begin this book with the conundrum that faces every gestalt therapist as they face fellow human beings in the therapy room. That in our individual uniqueness we can only ever get experience near to another, we can never completely and utterly comprehend the other's experience. To gain the best understanding possible of the other we need to appreciate the way they configure themselves in relation to their environment, the patterns they paint as they relate to their world and those they meet in their world, the way they form and shape their experience. How the individual forms and then moves on from one experience to another.

Many say that the word 'gestalt' should be capitalized just as any other German noun. However, gestalt therapy did not arrive in the English-speaking world yesterday. It has been here since the founders published their seminal work 'Gestalt Therapy' in 1951. One of its roots, Gestalt psychology was in existence for fifty years prior to this. It is clear to me, as Bloom, Spagnuolo-Lobb and Staemmler assert, 'it is no longer the proper name of a new modality. Gestalt therapy is one of many accepted approaches . . . and all are common name. Gestalt therapy appropriately has earned a lower case' (2008: 7). The German noun argument does not hold any water with me either as, 'gestalt is as English a word as frankfurter or sauerkraut' (ibid). So, throughout this book gestalt will appear in lower case[1] just as any reference to psychoanalysis, psychodynamic therapy or cognitive behavioural therapy would. Gestalt therapy has come of age.

To explain what gestalt therapy is in just a few words is a difficult task. I would summarise it as a relational therapy that synthesizes three key philosophies that have been described as the 'pillars of gestalt' (Yontef, 1999: 11), these being:

1. Field Theory: the person's experience is explored in the context of their situation or field (I will use the terms situation and field interchangeably).
2. Phenomenology: the search for understanding through what is obvious and/or revealed, rather than through what is interpreted by the observer.
3. Dialogue: a specific form of contacting (not just talking) that is concerned with the between of the relationship and what emerges in that between.

In the gestalt therapist's work these philosophies weave in and out of one another and the relational perspective is at the core of each of these three philosophies. Consequently, I see gestalt as a truly integrative psychotherapy. If any one of these 'pillars' is not being practised then gestalt therapy is not being practised. Gestalt is an experiential therapy and as such experimentation is key to the approach. The mind/body split so prevalent in Western culture is actively discouraged within gestalt's holistic view of the individual/environmental fields that are seen as co-dependent. The approach's radical view of self as process, rather than seeing self as something belonging to the individual sets it apart from virtually all other psychotherapies. As I said, to give a concise and adequate explanation to the question 'What is gestalt?' is not an easy task. The nature of the theory is such that it is not open to a fixed and rigid definition. Being rooted in field theory, dialogue and phenomenology that are all concerned with individual perception, it is not too extreme to suggest that there could be as

---

[1] Exceptions will be where I am quoting others who capitalize 'gestalt'.

many definitions of 'gestalt' as there are gestalt therapists, quite simply because we all have our unique ways of reaching out and making sense of our world.

I see gestalt therapy as a voyage of discovery. We are exploring how a person reaches out to their world, how they respond to their situation and how past and present situations impact upon their (and our) process of reaching out in the here and now. We do so whilst actively engaging in the relationship with the client as part of their situation, paying careful attention to what happens in the dynamic interchange between us. We aim to increase awareness through embracing the totality of everything the person before us is, was and can become. Gestalt is exciting, vibrant and energetic. Over the coming pages, backed by the ground of gestalt's substantial history, this gestalt therapist will continue to give his unique view of what gestalt is. So our journey begins!

2

What is a gestalt?

Simply stated a gestalt is the completion of what the founders[2] of the approach referred to as an *organismic* need (PHG, 1951), so named to emphasize the lived quality of the experience. A gestalt represents a whole experience that can span varying periods of time depending upon the need that is being addressed. A need to satisfy hunger may be met over a few minutes, or in the case of a gourmet meal may be lingered over, whereas a need to satisfy a 'hunger' for a fulfilling career may span many years. We human beings are inherently relational, it follows that these whole experiences are always formed in relationship with our environment. There is always, 'an interdependency of the organism and its environment' (Perls, 1947: 34). The diner and the meal inter-relate and one changes the other. When a need is met the gestalt is completed and the individual is free to move on to addressing new needs as space is created for these to surface.

Although a gestalt is a representation of a single unit of experience, I do not want to give the impression that gestalt theory suggests that we live our lives moving staccato fashion from one unit of experience to another. Gestalts are intricately woven in and out of each other. For example, as I am typing this an itch on my nose stands out and I move to satisfy that need by scratching my nose before reaching for my coffee to satisfy a need for a comforting warm drink (and caffeine). As I drink my coffee I project into the future thinking about what will follow this section of the book, before returning to the sense of my fingers to the keyboard. You will notice from this account that each gestalt is journeyed through in the present either through enactment or

---

[2] Fritz Perls has often been credited as being the sole founder of gestalt therapy. Although there is no doubt that he was a major contributor in founding the approach, the contributions made by his wife Laura Perls and Paul Goodman were also considerable and they are seen as co-founders.

imagination. The person's past, their expectations, the influences that are exerted by the situation faced and the cultural ground upon which the individual stands will all shape the way the individual forms and moves from one gestalt to another.

This process of an emerging need journeying through to completion has been described in a number of stages that have been elaborated and modified over the years since the founders described their conceptualization of a gestalt as journeying through four phases which they called fore-contact, contact, final contact, post-contact (PHG, 1951) – see Point 13. Many phased maps have since been developed and diagrammatically represented in an attempt to illustrate the completion of an experience (a gestalt). Two such examples are those devised by Zinker (1977) and Clarkson (1989) that have become commonly known as the *Gestalt Cycle* or *the Cycle of Experience* – see Point 14.

3

Creative adjustment

Imagine that you are on a hike in the mountains on a bright sunny day. Your attention is with the smells and the scenery as you amble up the gentle incline. The terrain then becomes steeper, more precarious as you walk across a narrow ridge. The wind begins to gust, clouds gather, the weather turns stormy. You adjust to these changing conditions by increasing your concentration, taking smaller steps. Your attention is no longer with the smells or the scenery but with carefully feeling your way forwards, anticipating the gusts of wind, leaning into it to maintain balance. You might assess the conditions as too dangerous and turn back. The situation is reviewed and reassessed.

As the situation above changes, adjustments are made in relation to the changing environmental conditions. Although we are not constantly climbing mountains, we are constantly adjusting throughout our lives in relation to our ever-changing environment. In gestalt we call these *creative adjustments* to signify the active nature of the movement as we create new ways of being in response to new situations. All healthy creative adjustments require making contact with what is now, rather than relating to a past picture of how things were. We take in the new information and form a new gestalt, rather than reacting to a changed situation with outdated responses. 'All contact is creative adjustment of the person and the environment' (PHG, 1951: 230).

Human beings possess an extraordinary ability to adapt to an infinite number of life situations. As we journey through phases of development from infancy to old age, we find the best solution to the situation into which we are 'thrown' (Heidegger, 1962). It is not that we learn to be creative, our creativity is a given. How we use our creativity depends upon our relationship with our environment; what encouragement there is, what permission to experiment, what restrictions are imposed. In essence, our ability to creatively adjust fluidly and healthily to changing situations will depend upon how supportive our environment has been in the past and is here and now. Other approaches describe symptoms, disorders or conditions. Although such terms may be used in gestalt we take the view that these are creative adjustments to a field that lacked or lacks support. We are always in relationship with our environment.

Every situation we encounter provides us with the possibility of finding the best balance between our needs and the environmental resources. Growth will occur as our capacity to renew and revise our responses when encountering novel experiences increases. Growth needs to be encouraged by the environmental conditions – a daffodil does not grow at 10,000 feet! Equally, a child does not thrive in an environment starved of stimulation or affection. Under such conditions the child may creatively adjust by compensating for what is lacking in the environment. For example, a child who is not held may comfort herself by holding herself; a child who is not stimulated may escape into a fantasy world. The child *self-regulates* in relation to their environment. The process of self-regulation through creative adjustment may be the best available choice for the child at the time, but may restrict the adult that the child becomes when they enter a relationship where support is available for a different way of being. New creative adjustments require the de-structuring of the old creative adjustments.

Problems occur when the creative adjustments made by the client that have been useful in the past lose fluidity in relation to the client's present situation and become rigid ways of being. They may become outdated and habitual, what are termed *fixed gestalts*, in response to a perceived lack of support and choice from the present environment. The present situation may not have been assimilated.

The process of creative adjustment is far from being merely a psychological manoeuvre. Our history of creative adjustments is carried in our bodies, elements of our client's histories will present on the surface of their being-in-the-world. A client who is over-reliant on environmental support, due perhaps to a psychologically suffocating upbringing, may collapse into the furniture whilst reaching out with bulging eyes and hang on the therapist's every word. Conversely, a client who is overly self-supporting may present as armoured in their body, not fully breathe in the environment and hold a self-supporting posture with muscular tension.

There are as many different creative adjustments as there are artist's brushstrokes or poet's stanzas but, just as in art and poetry, patterns and styles of creative adjustments emerge. The founders of gestalt identified different families of processes used to creatively adjust to one's environment. Collectively these processes were originally referred to as resistances (PHG, 1951). They have since undergone revision by contemporary gestalt therapists and will be discussed in Points 15 to 20.

4

Figure and ground

Many fine examples of the concept of figure and ground have been illustrated visually through diagrammatic examples (see below). However, I urge the reader to bear in mind that in gestalt figure and ground is used to describe any process of experiencing.

So what is this concept of figure and ground? Picture yourself watching a fascinating film at the cinema. The image that you gaze upon on the screen is the figure whilst the ground is everything that surrounds that image; the less prominent images on the screen, the screen, the cinema itself, the person sitting beside you, your journey to the cinema, what happened to you earlier in the day, your life outside, your relationships, the whole of your history, your cultural background. All of this forms the ground of your experience from which you create your figure from the image on the screen. Your ground will profoundly affect how you form that figure. As the film unfolds a couple on the screen embrace and kiss. Your fascination in the film may subside as sadness surfaces as a new figure emerges from your ground of a past relationship, or this may trigger thoughts that there is too much gratuitous sex on view nowadays with this reaction stemming from the ground of your parents' prudish attitudes.

This key gestalt therapy concept was first discussed and illustrated by the predecessors of gestalt therapy, the gestalt psychologists (Wertheimer, 1925; Koffka, 1935). The concept has often been illustrated by the depiction of a vase and two face profiles (Figure 1.1) known as the Rubin vase although many such illustrations are available. Figures 1.1, 1.2 and 1.3 show the relationship between figure and ground. One image cannot exist without the other and in all three examples only one image can be figural at any moment whilst the other forms the ground.

The process of *figure formation* is of interest to gestalt therapists in terms of what figure the individual selects and how it is chosen. In other words how does this person make sense of their world at this moment in time (and then the next moment and then

Figure 1.1 **Rubin's vase**

Figure 1.2 **Columns or figures?**

the next moment)? The figure emerges from an undifferentiated background of experience out of which focused needs and interests surface. In a healthy process of figure formation these needs and interests will emerge with clarity and sharpness, stimulating

Figure 1.3 **Old hag or young woman?**

energy. It will be a fluid process that will be updated in response to changing situations. When the process of figure formation becomes rigid or habitual, relating to a past environment rather than the here and now, awareness of the novel is diminished or closed. Consequently, the person does not integrate the new experience.

In relating to our environment, competing needs rise and fall originating from either an internal experience or external stimuli. As you read this book other figures will emerge as different needs/interests surface. A need for a drink may become figural from your ground, something you read may touch a memory, a seemingly random need such as a wish to contact a friend may surface, you may become bored, the washing machine cycle may be completed, the door bell may ring and so on.

In certain states, such as acute anxiety, figure formation is rapid and poorly differentiated from the ground from which it emerges. Assimilation of the experience does not take place. One blurred figure follows another as flitting attention leads to a cluttering of incomplete gestalts. Contact with the environment is diminished – breathing becomes shallow and rapid, negative thoughts and projected fantasies race, the whole bodily system speeds up. The person's failure to form clearly differentiated figures leads to them responding primarily from an internal pole, increasing their sense of isolation. Conversely, in a healthy process the emerging figure will be the dominant need at that moment and will be well defined, standing out from the background, what is referred to as *good form*. We could think of the difference as watching television with a damaged aerial and watching a television in high definition.

5

The here and now

In gestalt therapy we centre on here and now moments of experience. This is not to deny that experience has its roots in the past, or to ignore the existence of hopes and fears for the future, but these are experienced in the present moment. We focus on immediate experience and in doing so concentrate on *what* and *how* the client perceives their situation now, rather than digging around in an attempt to discover *why* they might perceive their situation this way. We believe that it is through heightened awareness of the way each individual selects and forms their figures of interest from the ground of their experience in the present moment that growth is achieved.

Gestalt's focus on the 'here and now' was borne out of Perls's criticism of Freud's archaeological approach to therapy. Perls asserted that, 'there is no other reality than the present' (1947: 208) and in collaboration with the co-founders of gestalt therapy, he developed a brilliant explication of the here and now moment at a time when almost all around were concentrating on the archaic.

In health the most pressing and relevant need emerges from the plethora of possibilities available to us. These figures flow one to another, emerge and recede from the ground of our experience. This process of choice takes place in the present and it is *what* is selected and *how* it is chosen that is of particular interest to gestalt therapists. Facilitating a client to explore their moment-to-moment awareness in the here and now can provide a platform for them to consider their motivation for making such choices, and provide an opportunity to reassess whether this motivation fits with their here and now situation. Behaviour in the present may reflect a behaviour that is causing the client problems in their wider field due to an outdated creative adjustment. A client who struggles to decide where to sit in the therapy room may be encountering difficulties in making decisions 'where to be' in their world, alternatively they may feel under scrutiny in therapy which may mirror past experiences. In this sense gestalt therapy can be seen as a microcosm of the client's everyday life and part of that microcosm will be the therapist's here and now reactions.

It is not the gestalt therapist's task to interpret or explain the client's behaviour, to do so would be to move away from the immediacy of the present. Indeed, part of the therapeutic task in gestalt is to focus on immediate awareness, to notice the subtle ways in which direct relating may be sidestepped through 'talking about' in the past tense. The therapist also needs to bring the full impact of their own personhood and be fully prepared to meet the other in the present with direct, here and now language in the service of the therapeutic relationship. However, although the therapist needs to be prepared to disclose the impact the client is having on them, here and now relating is not an excuse for indiscriminate self-disclosure. Any self-disclosure needs to be in the service of the therapeutic relationship.

I would like to invite the reader to take part in a simple experiment that I hope will demonstrate the ever-changing nature of our present experience across different modes of experiencing. Ideally, complete this exercise with a partner; if this is not possible you can adapt it to complete it alone, although interpersonal contact will increase the impact.

Face your partner and try to maintain eye contact. Check that you are well supported by your environment; that you are sitting in a supportive way, that your breathing is regular and relaxed. Complete the following three sentences several times alternating with your partner: I see . . . I feel . . . I imagine . . . For example, I see that you have blue eyes, I feel sad and I imagine that you are embarrassed. Your partner then shares their experience in the same way. Note whether you are tempted to rehearse what you are going to say thereby moving away from your here-and-now experience. Pay attention to the accuracy of each statement, e.g. When saying, 'I see . . .' check that you are sharing something that you can actually see, with the 'I feel . . .' statement ensure that you are reporting a feeling state.

Our perception of the here and now is only possible as we encounter change and difference. We need a background of the past to frame a foreground of the present for an event to make sense. For example, on a cold winter's day I open the door to go outside. My here and now experience is one of feeling the icy blast of air, yet this would make no sense without the background experience of warmth I experienced prior to opening the door. Fish do not know that they are wet!

> ... the present is not shut up in itself, but transcends towards a future and a past.
>
> (Merleau-Ponty 1962: 421)

6

Self as process: selfing

What does 'self as process' actually mean? Let me begin by saying what it does not mean. It does not mean that self is some kind of fixed entity that lives deep inside me.

Whereas other therapies and philosophies see self as a separate structure or existence, there is no such split in gestalt's view of self. In gestalt we do not believe that there is a self that resides exclusively inside me, only a self that is created in the process of me making contact with the environment. We make contact with our world through our senses at what we refer to in gestalt as the *contact boundary* – where 'I' ends and 'other' begins. It is in this *between* that self forms. Our selves emerge in the act of reaching out to our world at our respective contact boundaries in the present in an on-going, ever-changing dynamic process. 'We are the contact we make. We exist when we contact the world' (McLeod, 1993).

To more accurately describe this dynamic process in gestalt we use the term *selfing*. The use of a verb rather than a noun reflects the active process of the self's constant state of flux in relation to the environment. We are always selfing through a constant flow of creative adjustment informed by our history in response to the situation in which we stand at this moment in time. Our responses constantly change in relation to the situations we meet. If we accept this hypothesis it makes nonsense of any fixed method of diagnosis or categorization. I recall ending a paper covering my work with a 'narcissistic' client with what felt like a daring statement, 'during this work I have learnt that there is no such thing as a narcissist.' My client's history had been peppered with incidents where she had been objectified. When using descriptors we need to be sensitive to how the use of nouns will fix the individual in time and space, to do so does not fit with a gestalt philosophy. So, there can indeed be no such thing as a narcissist if we are constantly selfing, only people who behave narcissistically at certain times in relation to their situation.

As self and other are so inextricably connected, one cannot exist without the other. Hycner (1989: 45) suggests that rather than speaking of existence it would be more accurate to speak of 'inter-existence,' for we are all dependent upon our relationships with others to gain any sense of self. Hycner goes on to say that, 'There are as many "selves" as there are relationships we are in' (ibid). There are as many different ways of being as there are different relational situations. For example, I have a friend and colleague whom I meet in a professional setting but also in a social setting, our relationship has marked differences in the two settings. We are essentially the same people but the situation exerts a radically different influence upon us and we constellate ourselves in relation to this situation differently. As no two situations are ever the same our relationship is constantly changing. I would also like to clarify this term 'relationship'. Usually when we say 'relationship' we think of people, but let's think a little wider to include things, interests, actions and our changing relationships with these areas. I used to run regularly and to say, 'I enjoy running' would have been accurate most of the time. When I developed arthritis that changed markedly. Even prior to the development of my physical problem my relationship with running was in constant flux sometimes in response to an obvious reason, a slight muscle strain or having to face bad weather, and at other times for no apparent reason other than being in process with my environment.

Within gestalt some differing views on self have been expressed. Erving and Miriam Polster (1973) discussed a concept of self that involved 'I boundaries', which I see as a movement away from self as process and towards a more individualistic view of self. This was furthered in Erving Polsters' book, *A Population of Selves* (1995). These views do not fit with the wider held belief in gestalt that self forms in 'the process of contacting the actual transient present' (Wolfert, 2000: 77). As the Greek philosopher Heraclitus said, 'You can never step into the same river twice' and 'nothing endures but change'. One of the most important pieces of facilitation that a gestalt therapist can achieve is to collaborate in restoring healthy spontaneity in the self-function where that spontaneity has been disrupted or interrupted and is out of step with the client's situation.

7

The self: concepts of id, ego and personality

The gestalt concept of self as process involves three structures: id, ego and personality (PHG, 1951). These three structures are referred to as *functions* or *self-functions* meaning that they are processes that act in relation to the person's situation in the present moment. The way in which these functional structures act is as follows.

Id function

The id is described as 'the given background dissolving into possibilities' (PHG, 1951: 378), but what does this mean in relation to everyday activities? As you focus on this book other possible figures are beyond your visual field whilst vague figures also hover on the periphery of your field of vision; all are potential figures of interest. For these images to sharpen and realize their potential interest would require a movement away from this book and towards them. Likewise, the self is a collection of potential figures that offer the opportunity for numerous and varied sharpenings of experience, but they remain only as potentials until a figure is selected and sharpened through the ego and personality functions. Consequently, introspection will reveal little information about the id, which manifests through behaviour. Id functions are most commonly seen in situations of relaxation and also at the start and end of contact experiences. To return to you reading this book, the desire to do so will have been held as background at the fore-contact phase of the gestalt cycle before, upon completion, receding into the background again as out of your awareness you assimilate the material at the post-contact phase of the gestalt cycle (see Point 13). Although an observer may see certain behaviours as they watch us during id functioning, they would not gain a sense of who we were.

Ego function

The ego function is a selecting and rejecting function. Whereas the id function is a collection of potential figures, the ego function discards and identifies possibilities. There is restriction of certain interests in order to concentrate on the strongest interest, resulting in a sharpening of that figure of interest with a simultaneous fading of other potential figures of interest. These fading figures fall back into our ground and exist as potentialities for future figures of interest. We need to remind ourselves here that in gestalt theory only one figure can surface from the ground of our experience at any one moment.

The ego is deliberate, alert and conscious of itself as separate from its situation. As such it is central during introspection – we can be aware of ourselves in an isolated moment without being in direct contact with someone or something else. It is through your ego function that you are able to be conscious of yourself as you read this book. However, although the ego function 'allows for self/other process of the moment it offers no sense of continuity of selfhood' (Philippson, 2009: 66).

The deliberateness of the ego function in continually making choices is key in gestalt therapy. It is through the ego function that we gain a sense of who we are, but such a sense of self could be in relation to an outdated situation rather than the present situation.

Let me illustrate this process through someone reading this book. This 'someone' never had any books during their upbringing and was not encouraged to read. He was repeatedly told that he was stupid during his formative years, force-fed messages that were then reinforced by teachers and peers. He left school early and took on a menial job believing the messages from his past. Following a crisis he sought therapy and found a therapist who recognized a disowned intelligence. She suggested he read an introductory book on therapy and he found this one. He opened it randomly at this page, saw the heading and closed the book believing that he was not capable of understanding it. His self-concept formed in relation to the old messages from the past prevented any updating.

Work with ego functions is central in dealing with such *unfinished business*. A whole host of classic gestalt experiments, including the empty chair, were developed with the aim of resolving such conflict in the here and now through heightening awareness.

Personality function

The personality function forms a framework of attitudes and beliefs about who we are in the world and is autonomous, responsible and knowing. It is the figure that the self in process becomes that is then assimilated into the way we respond in the world. This process builds upon previous learning and growth. It is fluid and ever changing, although in what we might call 'pathology' change is resisted or restricted. Our book reader met with a situation where there was an opportunity to update his attitudes and beliefs about who he was, but instead he chose to close the book (and the opportunity) and remain with his belief that he was unintelligent. As the personality function is seen as the structure able to hold responsibility, it is this structure that decides the course of action to be taken.

I have outlined the different structures of the self separately, but in healthy relating there is a seamless fluidity between these functions.

8

Holism and the orientation towards health

Gestalt therapy is a holistic body-centred psychotherapy. I would like to invite you to reflect upon that statement for a few moments. Take note of your immediate reactions as you read the phrase 'holistic body-centred psychotherapy.' Now ask yourself the following questions: Do I split mind from body? Do I include spirit? Do I see body as an extension of my situation?

I do not believe that such a holistic view of what Heidegger (1962) referred to as our being-in-the-world comes naturally to many of us in the West. The term being-in-the-world is hyphenated to illustrate the eternal connectedness between our existence and our world. As such holism does not split mind from body, nor does it speak as though there was a separate interior and exterior experience or see a human being as divorced from their environment. Holism, sometimes descriptively spelt *wholism*, as the word suggests sees the world as a complete interrelated entirety. The founder of this philosophy was Jan Smuts whose work on holism nearly a century ago was later integrated into gestalt by the Perls, being seen as a process of creative synthesis. The philosophy of holism integrates well with gestalt as both see wholes as being in a constant state of flux, continually developing and evolving, rather than being static entities. 'The evolution of the universe, is nothing but the record of this whole-making activity in its progressive development' (Smuts, 1926: 326).

A well-known gestalt maxim that originates from gestalt's integration of holism into its approach is that the whole is different from and greater than the sum of its parts. This often-misunderstood phrase refers to the unity of human beings as complete organisms, and to the unity of human beings and our entire environment. Hence, gestalt therapy differs from many approaches in that it does not treat psychological events separately as isolated from the individual and their whole situation. A truly holistic approach such as gestalt does not exclude any relevant dimension in its approach, no matter how seemingly irrelevant it may first appear. 'Gestalt therapy views the entire biopsychosocial field, including organism/environment, as important . . . No relevant dimension is excluded in the basic theory' (Yontef, 1975: 33–34).

Let us consider the phrase 'the whole is greater than the sum of its parts', the foundation upon which holism is built. Think of your family and friends, past and present, and look at these relationships through a lens of support. Some may be supportive some not and all will vary depending upon your situation. We could embark upon a mathematical calculation and rate these relationships individually, add and subtract depending upon the levels of support or lack of support you feel, ending with a 'support rating'. If we did so the interwoven fabric of these relationships would be missed, they would remain isolated threads. We need to stand back and look at how these threads interrelate at different times in order to begin to appreciate something of the elaborate and fluid patterns created within our network of supports including how our supports are supported.

Gestalt therapists adopt a holistic perspective that includes the somatic unity of mind and body, the individual's situation together with all the influences that press in upon their situation. We attend to the observable manifestations of holism, the way the client moves and gestures, how they use their voice, breathing, how they fill space and how they situate themselves in the world which may be displayed in microcosm in how they situate themselves in the therapy room.

Embedded in gestalt therapy's philosophy is the belief that the client is fundamentally oriented towards health. It is through increasing awareness of their way of being-in-the-world that they realize their potential through discovering the 'answers' that lie within them, possibly buried under a host of outdated creative adjustments. We believe that there is an embodied wisdom in the organism to regulate to its environment in the best possible way given its situation. This process of *organismic self-regulation* is a central belief underpinning the approach.

The founders of gestalt aimed to counter the artificial splits created between mind and body through a holistic approach working towards the integration of the false dichotomizing of the individual and their situation.

... people are split up into bits and pieces and it's no use to analyse these bits and pieces and cut them up still more. What we want to do in Gestalt therapy is to integrate all the dispersed and disowned parts of the self and make the person whole again.

(F. Perls, 1973: 181)

9

Gestalt's relationship to the psychiatric/ biomedical model

The most obvious difference between the gestalt approach and the medical model is that the medical model takes an atomized view of the person whereas gestalt takes a holistic view, seeing the person as part of a dynamic field of relationships. The whole emphasis of the gestalt tradition is on seeing phenomena as working wholes compared with the medical model that sees phenomena as separate units.

In the medical model a human being is treated as a collection of systems (lymphatic, cardio-vascular, neurological, psychological, etc.) with exceptions to this limited way of viewing these systems more widely being confined only to environmental factors or other bodily systems that relate directly to the malfunctioning part. These systems or parts are vulnerable to dysfunctions caused by built-in irregularities and/or external damaging factors relating specifically to the dysfunctional area. For example, a heart condition may be caused by poor diet, lack of exercise and a family history. The patient is seen as passive; consequently an expert is needed whose aim is to restore the person's level of functioning to as high a level as possible. The level of functioning that can be achieved is largely decided by the expert and defined by a set of criteria that outline normal functioning. The expert advises any active role the patient is to take, for example physiotherapy exercises, otherwise the patient's role is as a passive object. Such a model is relationally objectifying. The relationship is vertical, meaning that an expert treats the other. This dynamic is evident in the language used to describe a medical consultation; Mrs Jones who is 'suffering' from depression is *under* Dr Smith.

I am not saying that gestalt therapists do not have expertise, but our expertise is relational. We aim to provide a milieu for increased awareness and central to that milieu is the expertise of the client. We believe in the client's wisdom to find the best way to creatively adjust to their situation. As such the relational stance adopted by the gestalt therapist differs greatly from that of the medical model; it is a horizontal relational stance (see Point 51). Although there are differences in power, these differences are equalized as much as possible. The medical model's relational attitude is I–It whilst gestalt's relational attitude is I–Thou (see Point 63).

The medical model describes itself as 'objective'; it does not value subjectivity and therefore is largely dismissive of human inter-subjectivity. Consequently, the patient's emotional response to treatment and the environment he is treated in are usually considered pretty irrelevant as long as it is sufficiently sterile. Administering the treatment is all that matters. I am sure that many of us have been in situations in medical settings where that is all that matters to us as patients too, but those situations pass and different needs surface that go way beyond being objectified as a condition. However, we live in a society where alienation from subjectivity is pervasive and given the character of this society the medical model fits well. A part of the field is the medical field and gestalt therapists just as any other therapists need to recognize when medical or psychiatric intervention is indicated. Thankfully some medical practitioners do recognize when more than chemicals, surgery or procedural treatments are needed.

Although the medical model appears diametrically opposed to the gestalt approach, there are some similar beliefs. As a gestalt therapist I consider that many psychological problems or so-called personality disorders/traits have their roots in the client making the best possible creative adjustment they could to survive an earlier unhealthy environment. If this developmental adjustment was made early it may then have become neurologically 'hard-wired'. As Greenberg (1989) asserts, this is similar to the medical idea that many modern medical problems confer immunity to other more dangerous diseases. One such example being that the gene that can cause Sickle cell anaemia was a lifesaver in Africa where it protected against malaria.

The differences between the medical approach and the gestalt approach can be summed up in the way the word disease is considered. Medically the word refers to illness with synonyms such as sickness, ailment and disorder. All relate to an internal experience. In gestalt the word has been hyphenated to dis-ease (Van de Riet, Korb and Gorrell, 1980) to illustrate that the organism is ill at ease and responding to an environment. The 'sickness' that presents in the individual will reflect a 'sickness' or disorder in their whole situation.

10

The awareness continuum

The awareness continuum relates to every aspect of gestalt therapy. The aim of gestalt is awareness, which is being in contact with one's existence and with *what is* at this moment in time. Implicit within this aim is the freeing of blocks that inhibit the flow between figure and ground experience. We can probably all relate to getting fixated to some degree on one particular problem that may cloud our awareness of our ability to process problems. A particularly distressing example of such a block can be seen in a person who is experiencing anxiety attacks. They may become figure-bound to their anxiety. It dominates their thoughts and grows into a powerful, all-consuming figure condemning the ground of their history of being able to successfully creatively adjust to situations to the shadows of unawareness[3]. However, the flow between figure and ground can meet with a blockage upstream or downstream. Someone with obsessive traits may be paralysed by the multiple choices that present in the ground of their experience and projected imaginings of the future, resulting in an inability to form sharp figures in the here and now. Similarly, it is easy to get lost in the ordinary rush of daily life with its various demands and plethora of messages about how we should be in the world. As a consequence awareness of our desires and aspirations can get buried under a mountain of externally imposed shoulds.

> The aim of Gestalt therapy is the Awareness Continuum; the freely ongoing Gestalt formation, where what is of greatest concern and interest to the organism, the relationship, the group or society becomes Gestalt, comes into the foreground where it can be fully experienced and coped with . . . so that then it can melt into the background . . . and leave the foreground free for the next relevant Gestalt.
>
> (L. Perls, 1973: 2)

---

[3] In gestalt we view anxiety as excitement that has insufficient support.

One end of this continuum awareness takes the form of highly attuned sensing or intuition where you feel in full contact with your environment. There is a brightness and spontaneity in moment-to-moment experience. The opposite end of the awareness continuum can be seen in those activities that do not require heightened awareness such as our ability to hold our muscles with sufficient tension through proprioception or during sleep where there is a clear need for lower levels of awareness. It is important that we do not put a value upon a certain level of awareness without consideration to the situation faced. Whilst the aim of gestalt is to extend the client's awareness continuum it is both unrealistic and undesirable for anyone to live in a constant state of heightened awareness – peak experiences need duller experiences to exist. Awareness can be vivid, muted, automatic, spontaneous, rigid, limited, blocked or interrupted and all can be useful or harmful ways of being depending on the situation. A mother may forget herself when caring for an infant. It is when that mother's children are adults and she continues to block her awareness of her own needs that it becomes a problematic fixed gestalt.

To practise gestalt therapy effectively we need to view the focus on awareness beyond a one-person process and see its emergence, subduing or denial within a relational matrix that includes what is happening *between* the client and the therapist (Yontef, 2002). If we only concentrate on the awareness continuum of the client we dismiss one relational pole. Our task as therapists lies not only with raising a clients awareness of how he is impacted by his world, but also in facilitating awareness of how his world is impacted by him *and* the process *between* him and his world. Such facilitation can be achieved through carefully considered, well-graded self-disclosure by the therapist.

There is a distinct tendency in the gestalt literature when discussing awareness to place a heavier emphasis upon sensory and bodily experience with comparatively few references to cognitive awareness (Fodor, 1998). This may represent the remnants of gestalt's rebellion against the form of psychoanalysis practised at the time of gestalt's birth. My view is that awareness is awareness whether it is cognitive, sensory, spiritual or linguistic and that a fully embodied awareness requires an integration of all modes of experiencing. We will all have our 'awareness strengths' as well as our areas for development (what we term in gestalt *growing edges*). We need to meet the client where s/he is with interest and excitement in discovering how they contact their world and with awareness of how they impact us.

> Without awareness there is nothing, not even knowledge of nothingness.
>
> (F. Perls, 1992: 31)

11

Individualism and field paradigms

As you gaze out upon your world, the complex range of attitudes and beliefs that weave in and out of your story determine the way in which you perceive the world. This story did not form within a void, it formed upon the ground of a particular worldview, and there is a story behind your story. This is your paradigm. It is more than the view upon which we gaze. It is the ground upon which we stand to gaze, the way in which we gaze and the lens through which we see the world. All of which will determine the way in which our bodies reach out to our world and the way in which our world reaches out to us. The lens through which the vast majority of us in the West gaze upon our world is an individualistic lens. Our individualistic paradigm is the ground upon which we stand and as such forms our cultural worldview; experience cannot be felt or formed separate from our culture. From a gestalt field perspective we can never stand completely separate from our inherited assumptions. 'We don't just "have" a cultural tradition, or the paradigmatic assumptions that underlie it; rather, we *inhabit* these things and they inhabit us' (Wheeler, 2000: 16). The paradigm upon which we stand not only determines our worldview but also our 'world-blindness'.

Paul Goodman (PHG, 1951) discusses what he called 'false dichotomies'. Man being separated from woman, mind from body, humanity from the natural world, art from science and the individual soul or self from a larger collective or spiritual whole. Culturally we live and breathe in a world characterized by separation and splits.

Gestalt's worldview does not stand upon such a paradigm but is grounded within a field paradigm where, 'the interplay of organism and environment constitutes the psychological situation, not the organism and environment taken separately' (PHG, 1951: xxvii). The environment and the individual (organism) are mutually dependent parts of the same whole. It follows from a field perspective that the individual's behaviour (acting, thinking, wishing, striving, valuing etc.) is viewed as a function of the person/environment situation, rather than explaining the individual's behaviour in a way divorced from the situation in which it arises, for example, as the person's *individual* pathology. In gestalt we are 'looking at the total situation' (Lewin, 1952: 288) rather than taking a single unit from the situation and examining that in isolation. A client may see herself as 'a depressive' but in gestalt she is seen as part of a whole dynamic situation and whilst the situation might have depressive qualities it is always in a state of flux.

When we talk of 'wholes' in gestalt we are not referring to a linear addition of parts. Wholes are organized as specific patterns of interactions and relations between all parts. If we remove one part from this field of relations then the part and the whole field will change. To fully grasp the dynamics of a process we need to understand, or at least be as open as we can to understanding, the impact of all field conditions. In the give and take of working with clients in gestalt therapy this would mean considering a broad range of possible influences that may reach far beyond any presenting 'symptoms' to what Parlett describes as 'The Principle of Possible Relevance' (1991: 73). This principle simply acknowledges that anything in the person's situation, no matter how apparently mundane or unrelated it first appears, has the potential to profoundly impact that person's situation.

If we stand upon a paradigm of individualism we suppose that a person's illness, disorder or psychological disturbance is a problem that applies to the individual in isolation, separate from his situation. 'That's your problem', might underpin this worldview. If we stand upon a field paradigm the view is radically different, the person is then suffering from his situation. Not only that, but his situation is suffering too.

12

The contact boundary

The contact boundary is where we meet and withdraw from our environment. Examples of our contact boundaries can be seen as our skin and our senses. However, if we limit ourselves to such a definition we do not take into account less easily defined ways of contacting such as intuition, sensing and spiritual contact. We also run the risk of giving the impression that the process of making contact is always initiated by us when the process of *gestalt formation*, making sense of our world, comes from the whole situation – both the person and the environment (PHG, 1951). It is in this process of meeting and withdrawing at our contact boundary that we creatively adjust in relation to our environment.

> The contact boundary is the point at which one experiences the 'me' in relation to that which is not 'me' and through this contact, both are more clearly experienced.
>
> (Polster and Polster, 1973: 102)

The term 'boundary' may conjure up the wrong image for I am not talking of a fixed point but (in health) a fluid, ever-changing place where we meet our situation and our situation meets us. Some diagrammatic representations, such as those illustrated in Point 14, can inadvertently give the impression that there is a fixed dividing line between internal and external experience – such is the nature of maps. I believe that a fine example of the fluidity of the contact boundary is made by Latner (1985) where he describes it as an event rather than a thing, and draws the analogy of our meeting with our environment with the shoreline's meeting of sand and sea. 'We would not say that the shoreline belongs to the sand or the sea. It is brought into being by their meeting' (Latner, 1985).

To illustrate the changing nature of the contact boundary in relation to our field I would like to invite you to complete the following exercise.

Experiential exercise
Make a list of six to eight significant people from different areas of your life. Picture them in a familiar setting, one in which you readily associate in your contact with them. Now consider how permeable, semi-permeable or impermeable your contact boundary is in relation to each of them. Do you let them in readily? Are you wary around any of them? Do you merge or are you resistant? Once you have considered this, I'd like you to 'shuffle the pack'. Picture each of the characters in unfamiliar settings, e.g. your manager in your home. As you imagine, note any change that may occur in your contact boundary in relation to them. Do you notice any softening or hardening? What sensations are you aware of in your body?

For healthy functioning our contact boundaries need to be permeable enough to allow nourishment and intimacy in, and sufficiently impermeable to maintain autonomy and to resist what is toxic in the environment. Consequently, healthy functioning is not defined by how permeable or impermeable our contact boundaries are in isolation, rather by our capacity to move along a permeable – impermeable continuum in relation to the present situation. At one end of this continuum is complete merging, what we refer to in gestalt as *confluence* (see Point 19) and at the other extreme, isolation marked by an armouring against letting anything in. Whilst these might be examples of the extremes of the continuum, degrees might be represented by openness or a tendency to agree, which suggest a more permeable contact boundary, whereas guardedness, defensiveness and being confrontational may suggest more rigidity at the contact boundary. Neither is inherently healthy or unhealthy. The ebb and flow of the tide of contact between self and other is always co-created in the between of the relationship.

13

The gestalt cycle of experience: early formulations

In *Ego, Hunger and Aggression* Fritz Perls proposed the concept
of the cycle of inter-dependency of organism and environment
(Perls, 1947: 44) in which he outlined a map of experience covering six phases in the process of the organism contacting the
environment. Below I offer an example of this cycle in relation to
an activity (my writing this point):

1. The organism is at rest
    *A task then emerges for me and I settle to write Point 13 of
    this book on my computer.*
2. A disturbing factor that may be internal or external comes
    into awareness
    *Whist writing this example my three-year-old granddaughter
    comes bouncing into the room demanding that I tell her a story.*
3. An image or reality is created
    *'Hell, my wife knows that I'm busy!' is my initial reaction.
    That then subsides as I make contact with the yearning face and
    wide-open eyes before me.*
4. The answer to the situation is aimed for
    *I decide to leave this work until later and put my energies into
    creating a story for my granddaughter.*
5. There is a decrease in tension as achievement of gratification
    or compliance with the demands result in . . .
    *The tension created by an interruption to what I had planned
    subsides as I reconfigure my field i.e. shelve my original task in
    favour of the new demand from my environment.*
6. The organism returning to balance
    The story is created and told.

With its roots in the above cycle PHG (1951) conceptualized a
process of contacting that journeyed through four phases. These
four phases in forming a gestalt were identified as: fore-contact,
contact, final contact and post-contact. The sequential process

demonstrates how the figure/ground dynamic shifts during the experience of contact. To illustrate this process let us take the example of the individual responding to a need for food.

Fore-contact – Excitement or energy surfaces in the individual in response to sensations of hunger. These sensations stand out from other bodily and environmental factors that remain background.

Contact – Following excitation the individual responds by contacting their environment and mobilizing in search of food, exploring possibilities. The desired food now becomes figure; the initial sensations recede into the background. In order to meet the figural need, the individual needs to alienate other options that may be present. This may mean alienating competing needs say, a need for affection/touch. The emerging need will then be refined; for example, the individual chooses between eating something sweet or savoury and hence sharpens the figure.

Final contact – Contact with the food is sharply figural as the individual bites into and tastes the food. The rest of the environment and the body will now have receded into the background. For a few moments the sharp figure of the taste of the food is the only gestalt in existence for that individual.

Post-contact – The individual feels the satisfaction of the fulfilling meal and digests it. The on-going digesting of the food will continue in the background – unless s/he has eaten it too quickly and has indigestion! The recent figure that called for attention has now faded into the background and there is space for a new gestalt to emerge.

To fully appreciate the cyclical nature of phenomena, we need to appreciate and experience the void between gestalts. In relation to the above maps, this void would fall between 6 and 1 in the first example and is the space that is emerging in the post-contact phase in the second example. When we let ourselves go into the emptiness of this void fullness can emerge. Consequently, this space is known as the *fertile void*.

14

The gestalt cycle of experience: later developments

Different phased maps and diagrammatic representations describing the phases of a gestalt have been constructed since Perls (1947) and PHG (1951) first described their ideas regarding a contact cycle. Two major contributions referred to widely are the Awareness–Excitement–Contact Cycle (Zinker, 1977: 97) and The Cycle of Gestalt Formation and Destruction (Clarkson, 1989: 29). Figures 1.4 and 1.5 are variations on these constructs.

In Table 1.1 I have given two examples of very different experiences and described them in terms of the phases of a gestalt cycle as illustrated above. One is an example of a need of thirst being satisfied, the other a conceptualization of a grieving process.

The examples in Table 1.1 and Figures 1.4 and 1.5 can give the impression that a cycle of experience describes the meeting of *either* a physical need (thirst) or a psychological process (bereavement). From a gestalt perspective the physical and the psychological cannot be separated. If I am thirsty there are psychological effects and if I am grieving there are physical reactions. There are completed cycles within incomplete cycles and this is most obviously evident in the longer gestalt cycles in our lives. For

ENVIRONMENT

Figure 1.4 Zinker's Awareness–Excitement–Contact Cycle

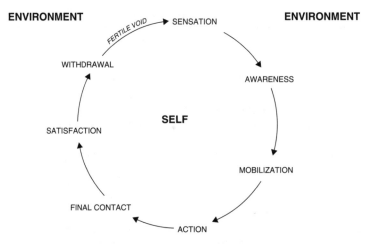

Figure 1.5 **Clarkson's Cycle of Gestalt Formation and Destruction**

instance, during a grieving process there will be certain resolutions reached within the process. Following my father's death my mother completed a gestalt cycle in her struggle to discard my father's clothes within an overarching gestalt cycle of a bereavement process that after fifty-two years of marriage will have many such grieving tasks (gestalt cycles).

A criticism levelled at the gestalt cycle is that use of such a map perpetuates and encourages an individualistic view of the person, and does not adequately address the impact of the environmental situation of which the person is a part. It begins with the emergence of an urge or drive in the individual and implies that first there is a subject and then an environment followed by an interaction between the two. In doing so it implies that the individual is superior to the situation (Wollants, 2008).

When using any maps or constructs in gestalt therapy we need to hold them lightly. They can be useful ways of conceptualizing experience, but they are only maps and the map is not the territory. All the influences pressing in upon the situation cannot be conveyed through any of the examples of cycles of experience discussed over these last two points.

In closing this point I would like to invite the reader to consider how their cultural background may affect their journey through

Table 1.1 Point 14: Gestalt Cycle, later developments

	Thirst	Bereavement
Sensation	Dryness of mouth/ throat emerges.	Numbness and shock response.
Awareness	Sensation is interpreted and need for water moves into awareness.	Reality of the enormity of the loss begins to surface with associated emotional responses.
Mobilization	Person moves to satisfy the emerging need, e.g. begins to mobilize self to get up to move towards a tap.	Begins to contact emotions in reaction to the loss – for example sadness/tears.
Action	Moves towards the tap, turns on tap, fills glass, lifts glass to mouth.	Moves towards expressing the emotion, e.g. eyes begin to prick, breathing deepens, lips quiver.
Final contact	Drinks the water from the glass.	Emotion is expressed fully. Cries, feels the hurt of the loss.
Satisfaction	Thirst is quenched.	Organism feels the force of the emotion expressed with associated response, e.g. relief, hopelessness.
Withdrawal	Moves away from the activity, the need having been met.	Organism withdraws from the emotion.
Void	Leaves space for further need to emerge.	Space is left for the next need to emerge in the grieving process.

the gestalt cycle. Having lived my life in Britain as a white male from a 'working class' Catholic upbringing with a strong work ethic, I experience cultural pressure to move on to the next task. Consequently, I can easily rush the satisfaction and withdrawal phases and struggle to leave space for the void. In my experience this is a common pattern with people from my culture.

15

Resistances, interruptions, moderations to contact

Different ways of diminishing or adjusting contact with our environment have been identified by Perls (1947) and PHG (1951) and expanded upon by, amongst others, Polster and Polster (1973), Zinker (1977) and Clarkson (1989). Originally described as resistances by Perls and PHG, these processes, which occur at the contact boundary, have subsequently journeyed through many different collective terms including: resistances, moderations, modifications, interruptions and disturbances. This can lead to confusion for those new to gestalt. In essence, they are creative adjustments that originally formed in relation to our situation at the time as the best possible way of managing that situation at that time. They are neither unilaterally positive nor negative but always need to be viewed in the context of the individual's current situation. We also need to be mindful that none of these processes function in isolation, all interrelate. One way of adjusting contact with our environment will affect all other ways of adjusting contact and our environment will adjust to us. For example, if I have a hostile way of addressing others I will influence the ways others address me.

Most gestalt therapists will describe seven inter-relating processes that we employ to calibrate our level of contact with our environment. This process of calibration in relation to the way we perceive our environment often occurs out of awareness, but can be performed consciously. I use the word 'calibration' here to illustrate that there are different gradations of moderating contact with our environment. Contact is not a black and white process, it has many shades of grey.

I will devote Points 16 to 19 to the resistances to contact that the founders of gestalt discussed at length and that I see as the core creative adjustment styles we employ in moderating contact with our environment. By way of an introduction to these four processes – known as introjection, projection, retroflection and confluence – I offer the following quote:

You might experience something is inside which belongs on the outside. This means introjection. Or, you experience something which is outside and it belongs to your organism. This is projection. Or again, you might experience no boundaries between your organism and your environment. That's confluence. Or you might experience a fixed boundary with no fluid change. This means retroflection.

(From and Muller, 1977: 83)

Having paid attention to the above I do not wish to diminish the importance of the following three creative adjustments discussed below. All have the capacity to be fine abilities as well as harmful rigid ways of being.

Desensitization (Anaesthetizing the sensing self)

The person numbs himself as in the acute phase of a grief reaction. In an emergency situation such as a car crash we may not be touched by the horror of the situation. Such deadening of our emotional selves assists us in moving into action, in the given examples to maybe arrange the funeral or call the emergency services and administer first aid – we act on 'auto-pilot'. Alternatively, this process could manifest in the psychological detachment from physical pain; for example, a hiker gets blisters but desensitizes to his pain until he reaches his destination. A more disturbing example might be seen in someone who employs a similar creative adjustment to survive abuse.

A degree of desensitization will be present in any addictive behaviour whether this is compulsive eating, sexual addiction or substance abuse. In our fast moving lives we can often desensitize to some degree as the pressures we encounter lead to us allowing insufficient time to linger over experiences and fully sense.

Experiential exercise
Take longer over your next meal. Pay attention to the smells, the textures, let the food and drink linger a little longer on your palate. Allow yourself to linger over the food, paying attention to your sensations.

Deflection (knocking away direct contact)

As the word suggests this process describes sidestepping or turning away from direct contact. Use of 'the royal we' is a classic example in which the use of a generalization lessens the impact of the statement. Changing the subject is another example and this manoeuvre can be subtle: a partner asks, 'Do you love me?' to which she receives the reply, 'That depends what you mean by love'. Deflection will often present in language; the use of 'we' rather than 'I' statements, the use of generalizations, stereotyped language, discussing the past when the present is of greater relevance, by diminishing the impact of what one has just said by dismissing it or laughing it off, by diluting emotional responses, e.g. 'I was irritated' when really I am furious. Deflective language will be accompanied by a bodily reaction to avoid full contact with the other – shallow breathing, lack of eye contact, distractive movements, shrugging off. Many of us behave this way when receiving compliments. Expressions of love, care or criticism may be bounced back, for example, when appreciating the achievements a client has made the therapist receives the reply, 'I couldn't have done it without you'. Energy is invested in turning away from direct contact, and we can all be very creative and subtle in the way this is achieved. As a therapist you may be alerted to a possible process of deflection if you hear the words but not the music.

Egotism (standing outside myself and observing myself)

The term *ego* is Latin for 'I' and in egotism I step outside myself and I watch myself. I am not fully in relation with the other, but am observing myself being in relation. This can be a useful process when there is a need to assess one's ability, for example when learning a new skill such as working as a therapist or driving. Most of us can probably relate to congratulating or constructively criticizing ourselves, this can be relationally constructive or destructive depending upon the situation. The process of egotism blocks spontaneity through control, as one *appears to be* in relation rather than *is* in relation. I can watch myself meditating but as long as I am watching myself I am not in the experience.

16

Introjection

> The hardest battle is to be nobody but yourself in a world which is doing its best, night and day, to make you everybody else.
>
> (e. e. cummings, 1994)

The process of introjection can be described in simple terms as swallowing whole messages from the environment and emerged from Perls' interest in the development of dental aggression. When the infant cuts teeth choice increases as chewing over what enters the body becomes possible. However, the environment needs to be supportive of this increased ability to differentiate, if force-fed by carers this selection process can be inhibited and the infant may learn to take in whatever is offered without discrimination. Such a process is not limited to physical nourishment, the degree to which we 'chew over' information or messages we receive will reflect in how we are in the world.

In introjection the person takes on board without question an attitude, trait or way of being from the environment resulting in the building of an internalized rulebook of shoulds, oughts and similar absolutes. Such messages are all around us: in our upbringing, our schooling, our religion and our culture. They are in the air we breathe and the ground upon which we walk. They may have been born from actual statements, e.g. 'Big boys don't cry', 'Don't be angry', made by people we can identify or through a process akin to osmosis. The person responding to introjected material, usually out of awareness, will feel a strong pressure to conform to these internalized rules and is likely to feel uncomfortable if they go against them. In our work let us not forget that this process will have originally been a developmental manoeuvre to ensure safety or acceptance and was the best way of creatively adjusting to the environment at the time. As such the client's creative genius stands before us, an energy that may be directed restrictively but an energy that displays the creative potential of the individual.

It is neither negative nor positive to introject per se. Introjection is part of a learning process, we may need to reconsider what we have learnt, but first we need to take on board that learning, and that may mean initially swallowing whole before assimilating later. When first learning to look both ways before crossing a road it doesn't really matter whether one introjects that message or not! Introjects allow us to internalize significant societal rules and to function within different societal systems.

Experiential exercise
Think back to your childhood. What messages or instructions were part of your daily life? What messages did you receive about your body, honesty, morality, sex? Now reflect on how many of these early instructions you still follow. Have you freely chosen all of them as an adult or are there some you just live by without question?

The process of introjection often occurs out of awareness in response to stereotyping. The advertising industry can be seen as a 'good' example of this – men should be strong, women should be passive, men should drink beer, women should wear make-up, men and women should be a perfect shape. I can also assure you that you really do need the latest gadget!

Many problems are rooted in a belief a person has about how they need to be in the world that has never been questioned. The person then continues to live their life by this prescribed way of being that has now become self-prescribed and can be re-prescribed for the next generation. An introject can support a whole system of moderations or, conversely, a whole system of moderations can be constructed to protect an introjected belief. People who habitually introject lack a sense of self and consequently are often on the lookout as to how they 'should' be and what they 'ought' to be doing. Below I have given an example of how a system of introjected beliefs can support each other.

Case example

Susan habitually attempted to look after me in sessions and would repeatedly check out if I was alright when she had contacted an emotion. She adapted to how she imagined I might want her to be.

We uncovered that her behaviour had formed in response to an archaic introject; 'Don't be who you are, be who I need you to be'. This belief was supported by another powerful introject carried from early childhood that led her to believing that she was unloveable. She had been an unwanted pregnancy and unwanted as a child, her mother had told her that she had wanted a termination. Susan therefore believed that she needed to adapt in order to gain a degree of love and acceptance. In order to live in accordance with these beliefs, Susan made the creative adjustment of splitting off parts of herself resulting in her disowning these parts. Consequently, she had never been loved for all she truly was. Through challenging her secondary introjects such as 'don't be angry' and 'don't cause trouble' she discovered that questioning was allowed and that change was possible.

If we return to the early influences on gestalt, one discovery that ties in well with introjection is that made by Freud that we humans fail to take in information or events that challenge our core beliefs[4]. We are capable of a creative selective capacity regarding what information we assimilate and what we distort, forget or reject in relation to these core beliefs. Challenge these beliefs prematurely, before a solid relational ground has been built, and they are likely to be defended forcefully.

---

[4] I believe that the term 'ground introject' as defined by McConville (1997) is more compatible with gestalt theory than 'core belief'.

17

Retroflection

'... whipping yourself with your own tail ... you achieve –
achieve just as well what you could have achieved without
effort.'

(F. Kafka, 2005)

In retroflection the contact boundary increases in rigidity through
an armouring process. Just as with a suit of armour the individual
protects herself from the environment and in protecting herself
holds her body back from contact with her environment. Whilst
this armouring keeps the environment at bay it means that
impulses are turned inwards towards the individual experiencing
the reaction rather than being expressed. Contact with the present
environment is resisted.

One form of retroflection is *turning an impulse back in upon
myself*. The individual splits himself into the aspect who does and
the aspect who is done unto. In doing so the individual substitutes
himself for his environment. This splitting is usually present in
the language used and is visible bodily in ways that diminish contact with the environment such as shallow breathing, muscular
armouring, restricted movement, paleness. I have faced many
clients who have given an account of being treated abusively by
another and when asked whether they experience any anger, I
have met with the response, 'I am angry ... with myself'. Here
the retroflective split is evident in the doer, 'I am angry ...'
acting upon the done unto 'myself'. Although, at one extreme,
retroflection can lead to self harm (F. Perls described suicide
as retroflective homicide), equally it can lead to self-motivation in
positive ways – I push myself to go down to the gym or engage
in positive self-talk to encourage myself.

There is a second kind of retroflection that is *doing to myself
what I need from the environment*, sometimes called *proflection*. An
example of this process can be seen in the process of rocking
oneself to sleep or self-soothing; masturbation could be viewed

through this lens. This process of providing for oneself what is absent or inaccessible in the environment can be a healthy substitution for what is missing, and if brought to awareness can provide the client with information regarding what they may need. However, if it becomes an habitual way of being that fails to be updated, in extreme examples such a *fixed gestalt* can form part of the foundations of characterological problems, particularly in relation to intimacy.

I agree with PHG (1951) that it is in the big, overt movements that we make in our environment that we run the greatest risk of putting ourselves down and punishing ourselves through the process of retroflection. Such a process of self-punishment can lead to humiliation, guilt and/or shame. If emotional or intellectual expression is repeatedly met with negative responses we learn to stop expressing ourselves fully. In the here and now of the therapy room bodily and intellectual expression is inhibited as the echoes of introjected messages support the retroflective behaviour. Muscles are mobilized but are held still with a balance of tension between the muscles that move towards and those providing a counter-force to the action – retroflection requires energy. If the tension held is enduring this can result in chronic soreness and joint problems as muscle groups push and pull against each other. This may present in subtle ways such as a tension held in the person's jaw. The therapist needs to be attentive to when these tensions surface in sessions. People that have developed a habitual pattern of retroflecting tend to restrict their use of space and lack freedom in their movement.

Below is an example of a dialogue between a female client and myself to illustrate one way in which the process of retroflection can be supported by introjection. The client's husband has recently left her for another woman, leading to her seeking therapy.

Client – *(Talking about her relationship)* He told me that he never loved me *(chest begins to redden, hands begin to clench)* . . . and that I'd never been a good mother *(fingernails now dig into her own hands)*.

Therapist – What are you aware of right now? *(I move the focus to the present to increase contact and counter possible deflection)*

Client – *(Volume of her voices increases)* I feel angry with myself for not having been a better mother *(Client's retroflective split becomes evident)*.

Therapist – That sounds familiar. Who would you be angry with if you weren't angry with yourself? *(I seek to facilitate some expression of the retroflected emotion)*.

Client – Somehow my mother comes to mind . . . but I can't be angry with my mother, she did the best she could. *(An introject that supports the client's retroflective process is verbalized)*.

In the above example we can see how the introjected belief leads to the retroflective behaviour of the client turning her anger in upon herself. In such examples of self-blame the retroflective behaviour is often supported by introjected beliefs. However, a failure to retroflect would result in a total lack of any field constraints leading to antisocial behaviour, anarchy, hedonism and narcissistic madness. Without the ability to hold back our impulses our society would disintegrate.

18

Projection

We don't see things as they are; we see things as we are.

(Anais Nin, 1990)

Picture yourself at the cinema. The image you are watching on the screen before you did not originate on that screen, it was thrown onto it from the film in the projector behind you. In essence, this describes the psychological process of projection whereby an attitude, trait or quality is assigned to another (individual, group or object) and in the process is disowned by the projector(s). In the previous point, I described a particular manifestation of a process where the client splits himself. In projection, splitting also occurs but this time the aspect is thrown out onto 'the screen' of the environment. Simply stated, projection is seeing in others what is present in myself.

Experiential exercise
It would be more effective to complete this exercise with someone else, but the exercise can be completed alone.

Take a piece of paper and write at the top the name of a character, fictional or real, whose qualities you really admire. Now list those qualities you admire. Turning to your partner (or maybe a mirror), maintaining as much eye contact as you can and attending to your breathing, I now invite you to share your list of qualities out loud but in sharing them own them for yourself with direct 'I am . . .' statements. Note any temptations to rush as you try the qualities on for size. Your partner may be able to offer feedback regarding whether they see any of these qualities in you.

Projection tends to occur when an aspect of the person does not fit with their self-concept. Examples could be seen in a client seeing their therapist as brilliant and disowning their own brilliance. Alternatively, one may attribute disowned shadow qualities such as a capacity for hate, terror or evil onto a group, a style of disowning that leads to all forms of prejudice and racism.

Sometimes there is confusion when discussing the concept of projection. One reason this confusion arises is because 'projection' is also used to describe:

- The ability to imagine what is not there – to anticipate a possible future, to be creative. An artist projects his vision onto the canvas; a poet projects hers in prose.
- The process where a historical figure is projected onto the therapist, for example a mother or father being projected onto the therapist. This form of projection is usually referred to as transference.

In the give and take of a therapy session a client could project their need or desire onto the therapist and then respond to their projection. For example, a client has a need for love and care but through a process of introjection does not see herself as deserving. She projects her need onto the therapist and takes care of her.

Before we go any further I would like to return to our cinema and the image projected onto the screen. Although the image may exist on the film in the projector behind you (though not in the form that you see it), it requires a whole set of *field conditions* to be seen on the screen. The screen itself is needed and that needs to be smooth and white to reflect the light. The cinema needs to be dark; the clarity of the image will also depend upon your level of interest and identification with the subject. I could go on. What I am saying is that the client does not simply throw something onto the therapist, but that there are a multitude of factors at play in the situation in any one moment. Just as with any other *creative adjustment* we need to view projection as a *co-created* phenomenon and recognize that this moderation does not occur in isolation from other moderations but that all moderations are functionally related.

Projection is marked by distancing. This can occur in relation to our own bodies and is evident in the language used where the body is considered an object of experience and not part of the subject (Kepner, 1987). For example, when someone is asked to describe their body experience they respond with, 'The shoulder is tense' or 'the muscle aches'. Here the split and projection is clear. However, the response may be a more subtle projection that suggests ownership, e.g. 'My shoulder is tense', 'My muscle aches'. The use of 'my' seems to imply an identification between body experience and self, but this is not necessarily so. It implies possession in the sense of property (my handbag, my car) and the distinction between the owner and the object owned remains. This can go unnoticed because it is such a cultural norm – and many therapists do it too! We may ask, 'Whose shoulder is tense and who is tensing it?' or simply, 'Who is tense?' Therapeutic work with projection of body experiences is a matter of moving from 'It is tense' to 'I am tensing' or from 'My muscle aches' to 'I am aching'. Beyond this the full figure will require not only connection between self and body process but also with environment, e.g. 'I am tensing . . . because I feel wary of you' or 'I am aching . . . because I feel isolated'.

PHG touch on projection in the form of prejudice. Perls recounts a story when a new candidate was being selected at a club at a committee meeting. At this club whenever a particular name came up and someone wanted to give them the thumbs down, the committee member had to state his reasons. The list of the members disliking the candidate and not wanting him to join the club amounted to a listing of the member's own worst faults!

If you were brought up in Britain you will have internalized some racist attitudes (Joyce and Sills, 2001). It's not possible to grow up in a culture such as ours with its colonial history and aspirations as a world power without having internalized some sense of white British superiority. If you are white a sense of white-rightness maybe deeply imbedded. If black, you may have internalized a sense of oppression or powerlessness or that other is more entitled. If you are black and a non-British resident this sense is likely to be increased.

19

Confluence

In geography confluence describes the point where two rivers merge into one. In gestalt it carries a similar meaning – a merging or dissolving of the contact boundary that leads to a lack of differentiation from the other. Such a lack of differentiation can be a beautiful and life-enriching experience such as when confluent moments are enjoyed merging when making love, the sense of losing oneself in a group or crowd singing as one, merging with your environment when completing a creative piece of work or feeling at one with whatever you believe in spiritually. Indeed, as therapists we need an ability to move in and out of confluent moments to understand, empathize and practise inclusion with our clients. A wonderful example of an experience of confluence is when we fall in love, we 'fall' from ourselves into the other. Whilst on the subject of wonderful examples of 'positive' confluence, let me offer another that I am less qualified to testify on than many women, that of the confluence present in the bonding process with a newborn child.

In the West the vast majority of us live in something approaching a confluent-phobic culture. Confluence will be seen in a radically different way within a communal culture. Standing on our individualistic ground, we separate rather than join. Consequently, and broadly speaking, I believe that confluence has received something of a bad press in the gestalt literature. Despite the fact that the notional line that it is neither positive nor negative is stated, what follows rarely backs this up. However, this is not to deny that a confluent way of being can be an unhealthy way of being.

The confluent person leans on the other as difference is denied; if the other person leaves that relationship they collapse. Should both partners enter a 'contract of confluence' their attitudes, beliefs and feelings do not differ, between them they may behave as if they were one person (Clarkson, 1989: 55). They may begin to dress in similar ways and even look similar. Confluence is marked by the proverbial 'we', with any conflict that threatens to disrupt the confluent system being avoided. Such systems are by no means restricted to couples but can occur in any relationship between individuals or groups or organizations including therapist and client. Where such confluence is present, even a relatively mild challenge is likely to threaten the existence of those involved. With a complete lack of friction there is a lack of vibrant contact in this low-energy way of being. The confluent person in 'going with the flow' may not end up where they truly would like to be, but they will expend very little energy in getting there.

A person who seeks a dysfunctional closeness in a relationship demonstrates an unwillingness to discover his or her own resources; a person who invests in confluence's polar opposite, isolation, demonstrates an unwillingness to engage in healthy dependence; a person who has the ability to flow with fluidity along a continuum between these polarities in relation to the changing situations they encounter demonstrates an ability to live healthily. This view stands in contrast to the notion put forward by Fritz Perls when he defined health as the ability to move from environmental support to self-support.

In therapy confluence can be difficult to break. The therapist needs to be aware of their reactions to this presentation. With the low-energy field created, one can become confluent with the confluence! Observing and stating differences, monitoring energy levels, saying what you see, allowing yourself to work spontaneously are all possible ways of increasing the level of contact that will act as an antidote to confluence. I also find it of great benefit to gain the story of how this way of being developed and in doing so gather a picture of what other processes support this style of moderating contact. After all, most clients that walk through our door may want change, but ultimately want to be understood.

20

Dimensions of contact

Although the moderations to contact can be a useful map when considering how we creatively adjust to our situation, they do offer only one pole of a continuum. When considering these processes in this unilateral manner there is a tendency to view them in a predominantly negative light, as something to overcome, rather than seeing them as a skill that has been developed and can still be of considerable use today depending on our situation. Some of these processes rest less easily upon the ground of an individualistic culture than others. This is the case with confluence and introjection both of which, broadly speaking, are about a loosening of our boundaries rather than a rigidifying or distancing which may be more acceptable in a culture that values individualism rather than communality. Consequently, I agree with Erving Polster:

> Yet, though Gestalt therapy theory broadly interpreted, is neutral on the health and unhealth of introjection and confluence, they have been almost invariably spoken of in pejorative terms.
>
> (E. Polster, 1993: 42)

The argument for overcoming so-called interruptions could be extended to the creative adjustments that we may consider to be culture-systonic as well as the above culture-dystonic processes if we view these processes as obstacles to overcome in a relentless march towards awareness rather than as serving a valuable function. The danger of such an attitude is that we behave as disconnected islands separate from our situation and each other. In contemporary gestalt we believe that self-awareness develops between our contact boundaries not behind them.

The following model based on the work of MacKewn (1997) better illustrates the need to develop a range of responses. The whole situation at the time will dictate where on the following continuums is healthy or unhealthy, safe or unsafe. The terms on the left and right of each continuum represent the polarities of that particular dimension of being; the term in the centre represents a marker for the middle ground.

Desensitization .... Sensitivity .... Allergic Reaction
/Hyper-sensitivity

Deflection .... Staying with .... Being Mesmerized

Introjection .... Questioning, assimilating .... Refusal to
Accommodate

Retroflection .... Expression .... Unbridled Expression
/Explosion

Projection .... Owning .... Own Everything
/Literalness

Confluence .... Differentiation .... Isolation

Egotism .... Spontaneity .... Lack of all
field constraints

When inviting individuals to experiment with different ways of being the gestalt therapist needs to be mindful that even the most apparently 'pathological' forms of creative adjustment were, and probably still are, supports. Consequently, when these beliefs about ourselves are challenged, the ground of our experience can shake with the individual experiencing a psychological earthquake if the challenge is over-pitched. One of the tasks for the gestalt therapist is to create a *safe emergency* where the client can experiment with different ways of being with sufficient holding. To do so, the ground of the therapeutic reationship needs to have been developed. Such experimentation will involve the client extending the above continuums but there will be times when it will also involve the therapist challenging their own 'comfort zones'. Both client and therapist need to lean into their growing edges. Within such a model healthy functioning is defined as an abiltiy to flexibly move along the above continuums in a way that is congruent for the person in relation to their situation. The greater our capacity to extend our ability to move along these continuums with awareness, the healthier our relationship with our world becomes.

21

Unfinished business: the Zeigarnik effect

In gestalt we believe that human beings have a natural tendency and a need to make meaningful wholes from their experience. Even if the whole is not present, we seek completion (Wertheimer, 1959; Koffka, 1935). The two unfinished diagrams in Figures 1.6 and 1.7 illustrate our need for completion. The series of dots in Figure 1.6 will be perceived as a complete circle, the unfinished '3' in Figure 1.7 will be completed. It is a human need to complete to make sense of our world.

The gestalt concept of *unfinished business* is concerned with our need to complete the uncompleted. Misattributing ideas concerning unfinished business to himself rather than the original work by Bluma Zeigarnik, Fritz Perls said that our life is basically nothing but an infinite number of unfinished situations, or incomplete

Figure 1.6

Figure 1.7

gestalts (F. Perls, 1969). As soon as one task or situation is completed another arises. These incomplete gestalts will range from the relatively trivial such as mounting housework, to major life events such as an on-going grieving process. It may not be possible or may be inappropriate to complete some unfinished business in the actual situation. However, if we fail to find some form of resolution we can become cluttered with these unresolved situations that then seek expression through psychological distress and physical illness. Patterns where completion is avoided result in the forming of fixed gestalts where awareness is blocked, satisfaction dampened, withdrawal avoided, impulses turned inwards and the possibility of allowing oneself psychological space is denied. Such processes can then become habitual particularly when supported culturally.

Unfinished business is also known as *the Zeigarnik effect*, named after Bluma Zeigarnik, a Russian gestalt psychologist who studied the effects of incomplete tasks on individuals. Through her research she discovered that unfinished business resulted in tension that in turn tends to motivate us towards completion. Her research showed that incomplete tasks take up more psychological space than completed tasks. She discovered that waiters with incomplete orders would readily recall those orders whereas as soon as the orders were completed they were forgotten. However, it was in her personal life that she gained a profound and fully embodied sense of the effects of unfinished business. In the following account I am grateful to the work of Elena Mazur (1996).

Zeigarnik suffered several traumas and unfinished situations in her life, including one major trauma that triggered what might be described as a neurosis. In 1931, Zeigarnik's husband was arrested, leaving her alone with her two children. She never saw him again – he was missing presumed dead. Zeigarnik found it increasingly difficult to live in the family home, a dacha just outside Moscow, being surrounded by memories of her husband and his arrest. So, in order to avoid her increasing distress, she moved to live in Moscow itself. Rather than improving her distress and anxiety this continued to grow. She avoided visiting places that she associated with her husband and this anxiety-based avoidance continued to increase to a point where she developed a form of agoraphobia. Her world continued to shrink until she decided to return to the dacha where she had lived with her husband and from where he had been abducted. Having returned she began to visit places around Moscow that held emotive memories of their relationship. The more she exposed herself to these situations the more her symptoms subsided. She had courageously and creatively discovered a way of achieving closure and finishing the unfinished. It is a key task for the gestalt therapist to facilitate clients to do likewise.

22

Caring and creative indifference

'Indifference' is not perhaps a word that immediately springs to mind when thinking about therapy and the process of helping others overcome problems in their lives. It is certainly not a word we associate with caring. However, in gestalt therapy we make the creative manoeuvre of remaining impartial; unlike other approaches we do not become goal oriented. As already stated, the only outcome we invest in is increasing awareness. The gestalt therapist believes in the client's ability to *self-regulate* in response to their perception of their environment, we work with that perception in the here and trusts now with the belief that meaningful insight comes from that which emerges in the client rather than that which is given by the therapist. In essence, the therapist trusts the client's process and trusts in the process that emerges between therapist and client. They trust that the client is oriented towards health. It is in their investment in the client's process and their indifference to any formulaic outcome that the gestalt therapist shows their caring.

Creative indifference[5] is an essential attitude in practising the gestalt approach. It does not mean taking a couldn't-care-less attitude but being open to each unfolding moment of contact in the therapy session without the need to rescue, pre-plan or hide behind a bunch of techniques or 'coping strategies'. Holding such a therapeutic stance means that the therapist surrenders to the between of the relationship and in doing so equalizes the relationship between client and therapist. The therapist's caring is shown

---

[5] The term creative indifference can conjure up the wrong impression but if we trace back its roots we see that some of its meaning may have been lost in translation. The original work from which Perls (1947) and PHG (1951) developed the concept, *Schöpferische Indifferenz* by Salamo Friedlaender (1918), was never translated but is better rendered into English as 'creative undifferentiation' rather than 'indifference', with its negative connotations (Wheeler, 1991: 47).

through their belief in the client to find the best way of creatively adjusting to their situation. This does not simply mean sitting back and hoping for the best. Being creatively indifferent means bracketing what you imagine might be a way for the client to progress to leave you free to move in any direction in your exploration of the client's world in the service of the person before you, rather than being attached to one particular outcome that may be gained from a restricted view of the client's whole situation. If we focus on one or two aspects of the client's situation they are unlikely to feel fully understood. Usually it is only when the whole person in relation to their whole situation feels understood that the fixed gestalts that originally formed to manage the situation at that time can be challenged, thus freeing the client to experiment with something different in the present.

The therapist holds an undifferentiated attitude leaving space for figures to surface in the between of their relationship with the client, rather than preconfiguring the therapy with plans and strategies geared towards a generalized picture of the anticipated presenting issue. For example, although a gestalt therapist might work with experimenting with decreasing the effects of a person's anxiety (they may also work with increasing tension), this focus would emerge in the session and the therapist would not invest in an outcome of, say, anxiety management. The gestalt therapist's prime interest would be in what the meaning of the person's anxiety was, viewing it as information rather than seeking to control it.

The therapeutic stance of creative indifference emerged from the Perls' interest in Zen Buddhism and the influences of Eastern philosophies (see Point 96) and involves both the therapist and the client facing the existential uncertainty of the unknown. It is fundamentally a position of non-attachment. The difficulty in taking such a position should not be underestimated in a world full of pressures to be a certain way. These pressures are just as profound for the therapist as they are for the client, particularly when we consider that most of us stand upon the ground of a results-driven, cure-seeking, fix-it-as-soon-as-possible culture.

23

The Paradoxical Theory of Change

The Paradoxical Theory of Change states that, 'change occurs when one becomes what he is, not when he tries to become what he is not' (Beisser, 1970: 77) and goes on to state that 'one must first fully experience what one is before recognizing all the alternatives of what may be' (ibid). Gestalt therapists do not believe that fundamental change can occur until there is a complete acceptance of the individual's whole personhood, including embracing aspects that the client may wish to amputate from their being. This simple yet profound theory has become a guiding principle for gestalt therapists.

The profundity of this theory is multiplied when considered in the light of its founder Arnold Beisser's life story from which it developed in true 'gestalt style' – experientially. I am grateful to Lynne Jacobs (personal communication) for clarifying aspects of his life story.

Beisser was an intelligent, athletic, attractive man, a US-ranked tennis player, who despite his many attributes was apparently ill at ease with himself. At the age of thirty-two he was struck by polio resulting in paralysis from the neck downwards. Having been an active, virile young man the only things he was then able to do for himself were to eat and breathe, and he could only do the latter with the aid of an iron lung which he needed for the first three years following his paralysis. Following an initial depression Beisser grew to accept his new life and developed The Paradoxical Theory of Change, which in essence had emerged from his personal journey. He was a sociable man, popular with others following his paralysis, his field of relationships reflecting his own self-acceptance. Even with his profound disability he was willing to support friends in any way he could. Towards the end of his life he said that even if it were possible to be given the choice of returning to being the athletic young man he was prior to his paralysis he would not take that option – he had truly become what he was and accepted what was. Apparently, prior to his paralysis Beisser did not consider himself to be a particularly likeable man. His self-perception probably wasn't shared by those around him judging from the number of people that maintained close contact with him.

If we concentrate on restoring what we decide to be health, we run the risk of depriving the client of the opportunity to live out the life change that is happening and to adapt to that life change creatively. If we attempt to rescue, we can rob the other of the journey to discovering the best creative adjustment to their situation. It is in taking that journey that the client has the opportunity to experience a far more profound learning than we could ever give, as in gestalt theory we firmly believe that there is wisdom in the organism (PHG, 1951). Having said that, most clients who come for therapy want to change something about themselves and their situation in accordance with some preconfigured picture that often involves ridding themselves of some behaviour, thought, disturbing emotion or attitude. If we collude with this impossible task, a counter-force can be co-created with the client who subsequently invests his/her energies in maintaining the status quo through outlining why that change is not possible. We need to notice what is obvious before us. The client wants change, they want something different, but they are sitting before us in their situation fighting to remain the same. If we invest in only one aspect of the client – their desire to rid themselves of the perceived unpleasant quality – whilst this may provide a short-term panacea we miss the aspect of the client that invests in being as they are. Consequently, we miss the complete personhood of the client – what dilemmas they are struggling with, what the change will cost them, the loss involved in the change and the value of that quality. Rather than exploring how to change or what coping methods may be useful, the gestalt therapist and the client co-explore what is.

During the years I spent working in psychiatry, I worked with many clients who experienced auditory hallucinations. Some were distressed by what they described as 'the voices' or 'their voices' but many were not.[6] Irrespective of the level of distress all were

---

[6] I would like to be clear that for some of these individuals their auditory hallucinations were so terrifying, threatening or deprecating that for

prescribed powerful anti-psychotic medication. The cost to the client of dulling down their auditory hallucinations was often a host of unpleasant and debilitating side effects. Not surprisingly many of these people tired of suffering dry mouths, constant tremor, drug-induced Parkinsonism, to name a few of these complaints, and discontinued taking the medication. Some sought different supports to discover ways of living with their 'symptoms' rather than fighting against them. Self-help groups formed and a National 'Hearing Voices' network grew. In essence these 'sufferers' accepted this part of themselves rather than treating it as separate from themselves and proceeded to creatively adjust to their situation.

According to Lichtenberg (2008) we cannot coercively change the other in some productive way. Such coercive change can only occur destructively through such examples as oppression, exploitation and domination. One must become who one truly is before constructive, true change is possible.

---

them medication to control these symptoms was welcome. I found that this was usually in the population that referred to 'the voices' rather than the more immediate 'my voices'.

24

Autonomous and aesthetic criterion

Fluidity is synonymous with descriptions of aesthetic criterion, and central to the gestalt approach is the promotion of fluid creative expression. The creative ground of the approach is reflected in its founders' backgrounds. Fritz Perls loved theatre and had worked in plays; he was influenced by Moreno, the founder of psychodrama. Laura Perls was a musician and writer before she became a psychologist and psychotherapist (Kitzler, Perls and Stern, 1982); she played the piano for years and had an active interest in modern dance. Both Fritz and Laura Perls were influenced by German expressionism and modern literature. They went on to collaborate with Paul Goodman with his radical views on social criticism that saw art as an antidote to what he saw as the evils of society. Through this creative synthesis of ideas, interests and ideals the founders of gestalt assumed that in human experience aesthetic qualities were inherent, evident in the human need to perceive their experience in meaningful, structured and organized wholes – to form and complete gestalts.

The term *good form* refers to a well-formed gestalt. In healthy functioning we creatively adjust smoothly to our ever-changing world. A process of transformation takes place as recently out-dated or archaically outdated ways of being are changed through contact with the novel in the here and now. A bright new figure is formed from the ground of our experience. Such a trans-formation is a unique aesthetic expression of our individual way of contacting and making sense of our world through the process of fluid figure formation. In the creation of a new well-formed figure we are performing an autonomous aesthetic act as a sculptor crafts a different form from an aged piece of stone. Both are aesthetic reflections of self-in-process expres-sion. The completion of a gestalt with good form and vibrant shape is a thing of beauty formed in relation with the environment

– a figure that emerges from a ground that holds a field of relations.

The aesthetic values of gestalt are articulated well by Bloom (2003) who describes them as one of gestalt's unique attributes and that 'the intrinsic sensed qualities of the forming figure contains the vitality of the organism/environment and is the radical core of Gestalt therapy's understanding of life' (2005: 54). In a lively debate with Bloom, Crocker (2004) makes the point that the skill with which some crimes are planned and committed, often with elegance, can hold the qualities of a bright, strong, vivid and fluid gestalt. I believe that such acts can give such *an impression* but struggle to see how a full gestalt cycle is completed fluidly and aesthetically without interruptions/moderations in full and vibrant contact with the environment in such circumstances. In such acts there is implicitly a disregard for the wider field, the individual concerned is likely to be responding primarily from individual needs detached from a wider sense of responsibility. In my book this is not *good form*. I do not consider aesthetic criterion to be sufficient in itself to live what most of us would consider to be an authentic, honourable life. Gazing through a Heideggerian lens (see Point 55), gestalts that are formed inauthentically have a different quality to gestalts that are formed through living authentically. Both will be creative but only one will truly be aesthetic in relation to the whole situation. It is 'clear that therapeutic processes that are informed by aesthetic criteria are important aspects of Gestalt therapeutic work. But these are not the *only* criteria with which to evaluate human functioning' (Crocker, 2005: 58, original italics).

As we have seen it is through the personality function (see Point 7) that I define who I am. It is through this self-conscious function that I develop a sense of stability through forming and maintaining on-going relationships and how myself and others can explain who I am if explanation were needed. Through the personality function acting in relation with the ego function, autonomy is achieved. Autonomy and identity develop over the course of our lives and the development of these abilities will be restricted or facilitated depending on the range of permeability and rigidity at our contact boundary in relation to our situation – how fluidly we relate. In this respect the fullness and richness of our development will be dependent upon the aesthetic criterion of the gestalts we form. We cannot learn how to be creative – we just are creative. Whether we use our creativity to nourish, diminish or destroy our being-in-the-world is ultimately our choice.

25

Support as 'that which enables'

When a client first arrives for therapy he/she is invariably responding to a lack of support in their field. It may be that it is not readily available or that it is not perceived as available but either way the felt sense is one of a lack of stability in their ground.

I see our tasks as therapists as being similar to the boy in ballet, we need to support from underneath, be alert to and attuned with the prima donna's movements, to show off her creativity and ability. If the boy does this consistently, the prima donna's confidence in the boy's ability to hold her will grow and she may gradually risk more daring and spectacular moves. Likewise, if we pay careful attention to the ground, the client will take care of forming figures themselves. Over time they will begin to trust that if they fall we will at least try to catch them and so the reconstruction of their ground will begin. Just as the prima donna perhaps didn't believe she could perform a grand jeté so the client may learn that anger is allowed or that they are loveable.

Laura Perls (1978) believed that in our work as gestalt therapists we need to provide as much support as necessary and as little as possible. This view does fly in the face of the misconception of gestalt as a unilaterally provocative therapy. This is not to deny the value of the ability to hold a provocative, evocative stance, as many clients will at times experience this as supportive. Another way of thinking about this is in terms of therapy as glue or solvent. For many years I worked as a gestalt therapist in the mental health services in the UK with clients who were particularly fragile or fragmented, many suffering or having suffered psychotic episodes. Often the last thing they needed was a stance that further dissolved an already fragile ego. I needed to adopt an adhesive approach that gradually built the client's sense of self. To put it crudely I saw my task as helping the client identify and stick the fragmented parts together. Conversely, if a client arrives with habituated ways of being that no longer match his current situation, a more solvent approach may be indicated. We may imagine that a solvent approach could be the more challenging. Whilst this is often the case, we need to be mindful that challenge and support come in many guises.

What is critical in facilitating the client's metamorphosis is that the therapist learns to fully accept that there is wisdom in the organism, that the person before us has the ability to find the best creative adjustment in response to their situation. To best assist the client in their journey we need to develop a range of authentic therapeutic stances, not as roles that we enter into, but as fully integrated ways of being. It is not only the client who needs to be constantly re-evaluating their creative adjustments. Good contact is only possible to the extent that sufficient support is available.

The gardeners amongst you will appreciate the need to prepare a fertile ground with the right conditions for 'figural' shrubs or vegetables to thrive. Even if we do our job of preparing the ground well, we will also need to take into account a multitude of other factors to support growth. Growth is facilitated through carefully attending to the ground of the relationship with openness to appreciating the conditions that press in upon the client's situation and the therapeutic relationship.

Experiential exercise
Pay careful attention to how you are holding your body at this moment. If you are sitting how are you using the furniture? Are you collapsing into the chair or sitting on the edge? Are there parts of your body that feel supported and others that you feel you need to hold? Just scan over your body for areas of tension for a few moments, maybe begin with your feet and work your way up noticing where there are differences in tension. Consider your breathing, something we usually take for granted. Do you 'breathe in' the environment or do you breathe shallowly? As you pay attention to these areas ask yourself where would I place myself on a self-support/environmental support continuum at this moment? Also ask yourself what your use of support may say about your environment and your relationship with your environment, e.g. the chair may not be supporting so I need to support myself, or the wider environment may not be experienced as particularly holding.

The client meets us with a wealth of information on the surface. A primarily self-supporting person may not fully utilize the support available in the environment. A more confluent person may collapse into their environment. The therapist's task is to discover with the client what the next step might be to extend their self-support/environmental-support continuum, in which direction is development needed and what is the size of that next step.

26

Contact and resistance

Good contact is the ability to be fully present with all aspects of ourselves – our sensing, emotional, intellectual, behavioural, sexual and spiritual being. It is not something that can be brought about through an act of will. To be in good contact one requires an open attitude and an awareness of one's ability for resistance. How we make contact is through seeing and looking, touching and feeling, tasting, smelling, sound, gesture, language, movement – the ways in which we reach out to our world.

Gestalt therapy's emphasis on contact can lead to misunderstandings, with a devaluing of resistance. Contact and resistance are part of the same continuum and both can be supports depending upon the situation. We are always in contact but we moderate the level of our contact through our ability to creatively adjust. Resistances can be seen as ways of self supporting and always need to be viewed in the context of the person's situation. I do not want to be in full contact in an environment that is toxic. Likewise a surgeon will need to diminish her level of contact with her patient – open-heart surgery is best performed whilst minimizing emotional engagement! Resistance to contact has its place. The gestalt psychologist Kurt Koffka gave a fine example of the value of resistance (Miller, 2003). He told the story of an outstanding German weightlifting team who were far superior to any other team at the time and were fully expected to make a clean sweep of the medals at the world championships. Leading up to these championships they were lifting far more than any of their rivals. The championships were held in a new sports centre in Switzerland and the team failed miserably. When a gestalt psychologist explored the situation it transpired that prior to the championships the weightlifting team had always been able to focus on an opposing wall and power against this 'fix'. In the new arena the light was such that a glare made the opposing wall appear to disappear. They had nothing to lift against, nothing to use as a resistance. This is also an example of how the field we are standing in profoundly affects the individual.

Resistance is a manifestation of energy and can be passive or active. It is often a way of protecting oneself from an actual or perceived threat or lack of support and as such needs to be respected by the therapist. There is always a story behind every resistance. Part of the process of heightening awareness is the telling and understanding of the client's story. In my experience accepting the client's resistance often has the effect of dissolving it. Some clients need to recycle the same resistance to contact whilst the therapist simply meets them with consistency. Others need to build resistance, an example being people who are too readily open in an environment where a degree of caution maybe indicated. Work with the contact–resistance continuum often involves many small steps.

> One cannot destroy resistances; and in any case they are not evil, but are valuable energies of our personality harmful only when wrongly applied.
>
> (Perls, 1947: 153)

By 'wrongly applied' Perls was referring to when a creative adjustment that was useful in the past becomes outdated in relation to the client's current situation. It is the actual current situation that determines whether a resistance is healthy or unhealthy rather than the style of resistance viewed in isolation. Forever the poet seeking the snappy catchphrase, Perls described our 'resistances as assistances' (ibid: 155).

Our resistances are created in relationship and can only be revised in relationship. We each shape one another's levels of contact and resistance. 'The reaches and limitations of our experiential worlds are continually being shaped in interaction with the experiential worlds of others' (Jacobs, 2007: 15). In this process of *co-creation* we literally create each other's worlds. In gestalt therapy we affirm and work with the contact–resistance continuum with the hypothesis that it is the resistance that holds the key to the future. If external support is not available from the environment and the individual believes he does not have sufficient self support then *impasse* results. This is when the person divides their energy between impulse and resistance.

27

The five abilities

A less well-known gestalt map but one that I feel offers an optimistic outlook are the *five abilities* – a set of creative adjustments to one's environment put forward by Parlett (2000) who identified them as: *Responding, Inter-relating, Self-Recognizing, Embodying*, and *Experimenting*. In healthy functioning – whether this be individual, small system, large organization or societal – these interrelated abilities need to be accessible to that individual/system. Whether they are fully utilized will be decided in the between of the relationship and will depend upon the situation, but they need to be available as potentials. When they are not, contact dulls, life becomes grey, relationships become detached – it is as if the fire that burns from the soul is denied the oxygen that feeds it. Through such self-restriction and due to our eternal interconnectedness we deprive others as well as ourselves.

Space dictates that I offer short summaries of these five abilities. I believe the best way of doing so is by offering brief descriptions given to me by Parlett (2007):

- *Responding.* The ability to self-organize in response to situations we encounter – including initiating and adapting, taking a lead and following a direction set by others, 'doing nothing' or stopping doing something; and to take responsibility for our actions and choices.
- *Inter-relating.* The ability to relate together in groups and as members of communities and also one-to-one with another person including dealing creatively with differences and conflict; and in general to relate to 'what is *other*' and different from ourselves.
- *Self-Recognizing.* The ability to be cognizant and aware of what we are doing as we are doing it, and more generally of how we are living and being in the world, making sense of our life and purpose and being attuned to our own development and limits.

- *Embodying*. The ability to experience ourselves as visceral, physical beings, who can be 'touched' at a fully human and feeling level, and can express who we are with all of our being, emotionally, physically and energetically.
- *Experimenting*. The ability to live in the present, exploring the possibilities and opportunities that are present, and to be prepared to alter or change self-limiting ways of thinking and acting as part of updating ourselves.

Given the ordinary language used in describing the five abilities, they are user friendly to the newcomer. They can also be readily understood by professionals in other fields of psychotherapy, inviting dialogue across modalities and a possibility of a cross-fertilization of ideas.

Just as a single moderation to contact or one dimension of contact cannot operate in isolation from other moderations/dimensions so it is that one of the five abilities cannot operate in isolation from the other abilities. It is like a football team, all play their part, but if one is not playing their part then that one will affect the whole team. Just as with a football team the five abilities can work together in an innumerable number of different ways.

If we consider the five abilities separately it is as though we are looking at our arms, legs, head and torso as existing separately, indeed as discussed in this section we are more than creative enough to live with such an illusion/delusion as we relate to our situation. On this theme regarding the five abilities I will leave the last word to Parlett.

They already co-exist, are joined up, each an integral part of the whole of a person's way of existing in the world; they represent five starting points, five windows to illuminate the whole (ibid).

Part 2

BEGINNING THE THERAPY JOURNEY: PREPARATIONS AND SETTING OFF

28

The therapy setting and context

For gestalt therapy to take place all we need is two people. However, the setting and context will profoundly affect the nature of the meeting of those two people. The environments we create interact with the therapeutic relationship – relationships do not take place in a void. For therapy we need a private, protected space but also need to recognize that any clinical space will have a 'voice' and some will be more 'clinical' than others.

Sophie is suffering from anxiety and panic attacks and visited her GP who prescribed medication to help her. It had little effect so the GP changed the medication and gave her a computer program that explained the physiology of anxiety and gave techniques for managing it. She gained some benefit from these techniques but her anxiety and panic attacks continued. The GP referred her to the practice's counsellor who was a gestalt therapist. At the first meeting her therapist asked her what had prompted Sophie to seek counselling. Sophie replied, 'My doctor thought it would help me with my anxiety'.

The setting and the context of the above meeting has preconfigured the ground of the meeting and shaped the nature of the relationship and the client's expectations. The history of Sophie's relation to the immediate environment is one of being treated primarily passively with any active involvement in her treatment being prescribed. The client's relationship to the environment stands upon the ground of an I–It relationship; her anxiety is treated as a separate system. She has now been thrown into a different therapeutic relationship with a different relational stance, but the environment still holds these associations.

In contrast let's say that Sophie sought therapy privately or through a counselling agency and sees a gestalt therapist in his or her own room. The therapy setting is likely to be less 'clinical' but other considerations are brought into play. There will be a greater degree of self-disclosure, as the therapist will have chosen the décor and furnishings of the room, the pictures and ornaments, if they choose to have them. These will all say something about the therapist. Part of the setting also involves the way in which the therapist decides to dress, which will also make a statement.

Take a few moments to consider what you would and would not want in your therapy room and what you feel would be inappropriate. What personal touches would you like? What about the seating arrangements? Would you have a 'therapist's chair'?

Any contact prior to the meeting such as telephone, e-mail or letter will give a certain flavour. We cannot be blank screens, not that it would be desirable anyway, but we need to consider what might already be present on the screen we present and the possible messages we can give.

The therapy setting needs to hold the therapeutic relationship, it needs to be sufficiently supportive for the client and the therapist. We need to acknowledge the ways in which the setting might limit therapeutic possibilities. For example, if I am working in a busy medical centre some cathartic work may be inappropriate or the size of the therapy room might preclude some forms of bodywork.

Clients come to therapy for different reasons. Most self-refer or are referred because they want to be, but some because the referrer wants them to be. The latter might include some form of mandatory therapy due to a certain presenting problem such as 'anger management', a management referral due to a work performance issue or a trainee psychotherapist/counsellor who has to complete a number of therapy hours as part of their training. Alternatively the client may arrive with unrealistic expectations that their anxiety/depression may be taken away or their relationship problem magically healed.

The context of the referral, the setting and the client's expectations all configure the relationship prior to when the client first walks through the therapist's door. It will be reconfigured again and again during the course of therapy.

29

Expectations explored, contracts established

As illustrated in the last point, one of the *field conditions* that will shape the client's expectations will be the setting in which they are seen. They will also be influenced by the way in which the therapist presents themselves; warm and welcoming, 'professional', distant, austere and indeed whether the therapist believes change is possible/likely. There will be many other field conditions that will shape the client's expectations in the present, a sample of which could be: their preconceptions about what therapy is, the client's sense of entitlement, what their friends/relatives think about the client attending therapy, their experience of change, their willingness to stay with uncomfortable feelings. In fact anything in the client's history could influence their expectations.

When I first meet a client I often use a focusing technique employed in brief therapy – 'the miracle question'. By asking the client what a miracle might be in relation to their problem I gain a flavour of their levels of expectations and entitlement. I am giving the client permission to be unrealistic – my internal response to many of the modest replies I often hear is, 'So, that's a miracle!' In paying attention to my reactions to any expectations aired I find it useful to reflect on the following questions in my notes:

- How do I experience the client's expectations? e.g. Are they realistic/unrealistic, modest, overly precise, ambitious, absent.
- Are they framed in positive or negative terms?
- Do the client's expectations reflect a dissatisfaction with themselves, another, a particular aspect of their field or a more general situation?

We do need to be clear about responsibility in exploring expectations. As gestalt therapists we do not give out solutions or seek to ameliorate unpleasant feelings. Unlike the prescriber of medication, we seek the meaning of the behaviour rather than alleviating it. Although this very process leads to insight, it may conflict with a client's hopes and expectations that somehow we'll correct the 'faulty part' of them and return them to some sense of a past equilibrium that no longer exists by virtue of them having lived through a change in their situation.

It is not only the client who arrives in the therapy room with expectations. As therapists we also carry hopes and expectations of our clients, some may be helpful some not.

Ask yourself what expectations you have of a client attending therapy with you. Then consider in what situations these expectations might be helpful and unhelpful.

Our expectations of the client will be evident in the contracts we form with them.

It is worth mentioning that some expectations may have emerged from generalized misconceptions about gestalt such as: that it is all about two-chair work, all about getting into feelings, is unilaterally challenging—maturity being a relentless march towards self-support, is concerned only with anger work and catharsis. Although any reasonably trained gestalt therapist would agree that these notions are hopelessly inaccurate, such ideas do jangle around the field and can shape expectations.

Contracts

I find the word 'contracts' such an officious term to use when working with people's distress. However, an agreement between therapist and client is needed as part of the holding environment. All the intricacies of contracts cannot be fully addressed here but that said I see contracts as covering three broad areas.

1. The 'Business' contract

This covers the 'nuts and bolts' of the agreement to meet and serves to clarify the business end of therapy. Included in this contract are areas such as: length of sessions, fees (if applicable), number of sessions or review intervals, notice required for cancellation

and terminating therapy, the code of ethics the therapist abides by
(UKCP, BACP[7], etc.).

In this contract we will also outline the limits of confidentiality,
which are as follows:

(a) Confidentiality would need to be broken if the client becomes
    a danger to themselves or others. This would be in accord-
    ance with such legal requirements as The Mental Health Act,
    The Child Protection Act, Terrorism Act, and Data Protec-
    tion Act. However, and I would like to stress this point (as I
    often do with clients), there is a world of difference between
    someone having thoughts of harming themselves or others
    and acting upon those thoughts.
(b) It is an ethical requirement in the UK that therapists are in
    regular clinical supervision which means that the therapist
    will discuss with their clinical supervisor the content of ses-
    sions (see Point 94). This is something of a 'quality assurance
    policy'. It also guards against therapists working through
    their own issues via the client, and so also acts as an 'insur-
    ance policy'.
(c) If I was required to give information by a Court of Law.

2. The Therapy contract

The very nature of gestalt therapy is of unfolding awareness in
relation to the client's field of relationships. A hard and fast therapy contract that sticks doggedly to one agreed area does not fit
with the gestalt approach or the twists and turns of human relating. Whilst we need sufficient flexibility to allow for the exploration of experiences that may appear tangential to a presenting
issue, we also need to strike a balance in being sufficiently focused.
The situation in which we meet with a client will influence the
nature of the therapy contract. For example, if we have a limited
number of sessions then deciding upon the direction of the therapy is likely to be more figural than if the therapy is open ended
where more time can be spent with emerging needs. However, as a

---

[7] United Kingdom Council for Psychotherapy, British Association for
Counselling and Psychotherapy.

process therapy, any therapy contract needs to allow for sufficient flexibility to allow for the exploration of seemingly unrelated events that are likely to reveal a pattern of relating.

3. Therapeutic boundaries

I will address therapeutic boundaries in the section discussing Ethics and Values. Suffice to say here that, as for any of the afore-mentioned areas, contracts need to be made with an attitude of care, holding the possibility of flexibility in response to a thera-peutic need. If not we run the risk of an outdated contract lead-ing the therapy rather than re-evaluating the changing situation between the client and their world together with the developing client–therapist relationship.

30

Listening to the client's story

The world may be made of atoms but it is held together by stories. We create a narrative about ourselves that gives us a sense of who we are in the world, what is and is not possible for us. These stories are not created merely through a cognitive process but are embodied senses of who we are. Our personal narrative will reveal itself through the way we hold ourselves, walk, move, and through all our *contact functions* – the way in which we make contact in the world. If my personal narrative is one of a lack of entitlement I may be tentative in my actions, anxious when meeting people I perceive as superior, restricted in my ambitions. There will be many ways of being that will fit within the frame of the story I tell myself and to reach outside of these restrictions will mean creating a new self-narrative. A person's narrative and the way in which they organize themselves in the world begins to unfold from the first moment of meeting. A client's protective grandiosity, a sense of shame at coming to therapy or a retroflective body armour are likely to be seen or sensed before they are given a voice.

It is not only the telling of a person's story that is a whole body experience. Anyone whose heart has felt heavy or whose eyes have prickled when hearing another's experience will know that in listening to another's story it is more than just the ear drum that resonates. Listening is an embodied experience. If there is a lack of resonance or the client does not impact you, treat this as information. It might be information primarily about you, the therapist, responding to your own material or you may be experiencing a transference reaction in response to the client's way of being (see Point 36).

One of the prime needs for any human being is to be understood and telling our story is a way of facilitating that yearned-for understanding. I often begin a first session with a client with a simple request, 'Tell me your story'. In telling their story the client reveals a gestalt of their experience perhaps incomplete, often unfinished frequently outdated.

Our ability to express ourselves verbally through language broadens the ways in which we can *be with* another. It allows us to construct a narrative and affords the opportunity of making our experience more shareable. Two people (or more) can create mutual experiences of meaning. However, our ability to use language is double-edged. Whilst language provides a vehicle for sharing experience it also makes part of our known experience less shareable. 'It drives a wedge between two simultaneous forms of interpersonal experience: as it is lived and as it is verbally expressed' (Stern, 1998: 163). Our experiences and felt senses can only be partially expressed through language, which in our culture is invariably elevated to a higher level of accurate expression than other modes of expression. It is in fact a less accurate form, as language moves our relating away from the personal immediate level of communication onto a more impersonal abstract level. Words are an approximate description of one's experience and may hold a different meaning for the other yet to be taken as truth.

The wonderfully entitled book *Every Person's Life is Worth a Novel* by Erving Polster (1987) for me sums up the uniqueness and intricateness of each person's story. When listening to that story we need to begin by exploring how the client experiences herself in relation to her situation. We need to give the client sufficient space so that she can engage in organizing herself and we need to listen with our whole being.

31

Process diagnosis

Diagnosis and therapy are the same process.

(PHG, 1951: 230)

The term 'diagnosis' holds controversy for many gestalt therapists with its objectifying relational stance. However, our human need to make meaning of our world means that it is inevitable that we will diagnose. Also, as Delisle states,

... maintaining that diagnosis is depersonalizing, perhaps we have forgotten that it is as depersonalizing, anti-therapeutic and repressive to deny the existence of real differences between individuals.

(Delisle, 1999: 10)

What we need to hold in our awareness is that human beings and the whole field are fluid and ever changing. From a gestalt perspective we need to diagnose the person within their situation taking into account all the relevant conditions that impact the way in which the person perceives their field. We also need to have sufficient awareness of our own process and biases. The therapist's personality traits and interpersonal relational patterns need to be taken into consideration with regards to how their way of being may impact the client. In making a process diagnosis of the person in relation to their situation, it follows that any diagnosis will be a temporary assessment at one moment in time. A series of these moments over time will give an impression of a pattern of relating, but let us not forget that patterns change and that reality and meaning are co-created. Process diagnosis should offer a possible direction to a 'treatment' that is flexible to changes in the situation – if I wear my reading glasses to walk down the street they are more of a hindrance than help.

Diagnosis is the application of theoretical constructs to create a shorthand picture of how one makes and breaks contact with their world. In diagnosing through, for example, applying one or more of the maps in the preceding section, even if we make our diagnosis as relational as possible, the very nature of the process of applying a theoretical construct that offers a shorthand hypothesis means that parts of the story get missed. The map is not the territory; diagnostic maps simplify as much as they mimic the world and cannot account for everything that comes into existence between client and therapist.

'To diagnose means to observe and assess the person–world situation' (Wollants, 2008: 76). This assessment involves looking at the figural aspects that are impacting upon that person's world from that person's perspective whilst holding that any number of different figures may surface from the ground of their experience rendering the original diagnosis redundant. Within our individualistic culture what are often considered personal conflicts are really interpersonal-situational conflicts of which the person is but a part. Behaviour has a function and we can only begin to understand its function if we consider it within the context of the person's whole situation. If we do so the function may be understood rather than labelled.

Many therapists, including gestalt therapists, use psychiatric terms freely, particularly those relating to personality 'disorders' or traits. Whilst these maps can be useful and help therapists to treatment-plan and dialogue with other related professions, casual use of such fixed terms runs the risk of pathologizing one pole of the relationship. Terms such as narcissist, borderline or depressive fix the client in time and space. To remain true to our belief that our selves are fluid and ever changing in relation to the situations we meet and perceive we need to make any descriptors relational by describing them as verbs rather than nouns.

In considering how a process of diagnosis rests with gestalt's phenomenological field perspective, I come to the following conclusions that:

1. Any process of diagnosis needs to have an emphasis on description and be *phenomenological*.
2. Any diagnosis needs to recognize the impact of the wider situation.

3. Process language (such as the use of verbs rather than nouns) should be used to illustrate the flexible nature of the diagnosis.
4. Any process of diagnosis I engage in will be heavily influenced by how I make sense of the situation.
5. During the I–It process of diagnosis I need to hold an I–Thou relational attitude (see Point 72).

32

Assessment

Assessment and diagnosis go hand in hand. So what do we assess? In essence, how the client makes and breaks contact. We assess the client's way of being in the present in relation to their presenting issue. We might think of assessment as something that happens at the initial meeting, but just as with the process of diagnosis assessment needs to be an on-going process. However, initial assessment does differ from on-going assessment, there is certain ground that needs to be covered during the first few meetings and a greater degree of structure is needed particularly if there are field constraints such as a limited number of sessions available. The following is a suggestion of a broad outline to a structure:

1. Identify the presenting issue – What has brought the client to therapy and why now?
2. In response to the client's way of being and reporting of their presenting issue begin to formulate some *possible* ideas around how this issue *may* have developed and/or be maintained. Do hold your hypotheses loosely.
3. Explore the client's expectations for therapy and work towards identifying possible goals.
4. With the client begin to construct a possible way forward to achieving their goals. This may include giving an outline of the nature of gestalt therapy, explaining that it is a process-focused therapy rather than an outcome-oriented therapy.
5. A crucial part of the assessment is to consider whether you are the right person to assist this person and whether gestalt might be a suitable approach. Is the nature of the therapy likely to be within our level of competency?
6. We need to assess any risk issues to self and/or others (see Point 89).

Just as in the process of diagnosis, assessment will be most effective if it is descriptive, dynamic and fluid and underpinned by the belief that any reality is co-created. Although gestalt is renowned for focusing on the *here and now*, it is important to gain a context and history. By inquiring about the client's *there and then* experience, both recent and archaic, we gain some indication of fixed gestalts and transferential possibilities (see Point 36). Also, if the therapist pays close attention to their own reactions to the client (emotional response, emerging thoughts, 'negative' reactions, etc.) this can be a source of valuable information as long as the therapist is vigilant in separating out their own proactive material. We also need to hold an awareness of any power imbalances in relation to difference, in addition to the existing client/ therapist imbalance.

We consider how the client's pattern of making and breaking contact in the session reflects their presenting story. For instance, a client has given an account of an abusive background:

Susan has come to therapy complaining of dissatisfaction in her relationships. She describes an abusive upbringing in which it was unsafe for her to express strong emotions. She sits rigidly in the chair as she tells her evocative story with little emotion; on the occasions when she seems to become more animated she swallows, as if swallowing down an emerging feeling. Her breathing is shallow; her complexion pale as she tells how she had to hold in her feelings as a child and that she still does today. Her therapist is getting a picture of a retroflective process supported by introjected beliefs around non-expression of emotion. He wonders how he and the therapy situation might be contributing to this.

Delisle (1999) offers a template for initial and on-going assessment covering, amongst others, the following areas of inquiry: how the client makes contact, moves, uses support in the session and how they use daily support outside. Delisle's work will be discussed further in Point 34.

It is useful to ask what a client wants from therapy even though many clients struggle with this simple question. Any struggle in itself will give information, however we may choose to assist the client through experimenting with projecting into the future.

Looking through a support lens we may map the client's existing supports and ask what sort of support would be needed to achieve any desired change whilst noting how the client reaches out or struggles to reach out in the here and now of the therapy session both verbally and bodily.

33

The client's situation

The client's situation is their unique experience of their field including how they are impacted by and how they impact their environment. Fritz Perls (1947; PHG, 1951) emphasized that humans endow meaning to aspects of their environment and that meaning will be unique to that individual at that point in time. Through dialogue, careful phenomenological inquiry and appreciation of the way the client reaches out to his world – and how his world touches him – with skill, emotional engagement and patience we can gain an impression of their situation, but we can never actually experience their situation.

Let me be clear that the client's situation is not something *out there*, even before a client walks through our door we become a part of their situation as they begin to think about therapy and move towards setting it up. We do not see the person in some detached, atomized way separate from their world. In field theory, which we could re-brand as *situation theory*, we believe that any part of a system affects the whole system. We cannot work with the client and the client's situation separately. The whole determines the parts and it is only the interplay between organism and environment that constitutes the psychological situation, not the organism and the environment taken separately (PHG, 1951).

Gestalt therapy deals with 'wholes' and the properties of the whole are emergent. Through this emergent process something comes into being as a result of the constituent parts that make up the whole coming together that none of those constituent parts carry in isolation. Simplistically, we might think of this in terms of the old saying 'the straw that broke the camel's back'. It is not actually that one final straw that broke the camel's back and nor could any of the other 'straws' have broken it alone. There will also be a host of other field conditions that contribute towards incapacitating our poor camel, e.g. diet, its treatment by its owner, hereditary factors, its gait and proprioception. Hopefully it is not a giant leap to see how the client's whole situation might impact the visible and disturbing presenting fragment (their depression, anxiety, relationship problem) seen on the surface. What is there in the client's ground that supports the figural problem and what new supports might now be needed in their current situation? In the language of gestalt we refer to the restoration of a sense of equilibrium as *good form*, where figures have clarity, having emerged from, and being supported by, a solid ground.

Although the client's situation is present *here and now* this is not an isolated unit of experience. The moments in a gestalt therapy session do not stand in isolation from each other and nor does a session take place within a void. We cannot detach the client from their experience of what they are living through beyond the therapy room. Yontef (1988) discussed four space/time zones all of which are key to the client's situation:

- The *here and now* – see Point 5.
- The *there and now* – This is specifically concerned with how the client's environmental field, their *lifespace* impacts upon the present situation and how the client's relationships are constellated in the present situation.
- The *here and then* – The therapeutic context of the meeting. It is concerned with the ground of your relationship with the client and the patterns that shape your relationship over time. Possible *here and then* influences include the location of the therapy (doctor's surgery, private practice, etc.), how the therapist has advertised herself.
- The *there and then* – Includes the client's developmental history, their life story. As therapists an awareness of the client's history can assist us in understanding how current relationships are constellated.

In the give and take of a gestalt therapy session the above time/space zones weave in and out of each other and, as they do, so add colour and shape to the client's situation. In practising gestalt therapy one of the most important points we need to hold in relation to the client facing us is that they are part of a larger whole, part of a multitudinous field of relations. This relational matrix supports their situation, but let us not be daunted for the next step lies on the surface waiting to unfold in relationship.

34

The client's contact functions

We achieve contact with our environment through what we term in gestalt as *contact functions*. In essence, they describe the five senses together with how we move and hold ourselves in relation to our world. Without effective contact choiceful awareness is not possible. We can never be out of contact completely. There are degrees of contact and avoidance of contact and these can only be assessed in the context of the situation. Client and therapist may moderate their contact more in an initial session, as there is likely to be increased anxiety in meeting the unfamiliar.

Polster and Polster (1973) listed the contact functions as, looking, listening, touching, talking, moving, smelling and tasting. Delisle (1999) developed a set of questions designed to provide a subjective assessment of the client's observable contact functions. Questions that may prove fruitful in initial and on-going assessment covering the client's observable contact functions are as follows:

- *Looking/Seeing Contact Function*
  When does the client look at you and when does the client look away from you?
  How do you feel about the way in which the client looks at you?
  How would you describe this person's eyes and the way in which they look?
  What emotions do I feel that these eyes would most easily express?
- *Voice/Speech Contact Function*
  How would I describe this person's voice?
  What do I feel in response to this voice and what emotions do I imagine this voice best expresses?
  How does this person use their voice?
- *Listening/Hearing Contact Function*
  Does this person seem to hear me easily?
  Does this person hear something other than what I say?

> Do I feel that it is easy to be heard and understood by this person?

- *Touch/Movement Contact Function*
  What do I imagine I would feel if this person touched me?
  What do I imagine we would each feel if I were to touch them?
  Would I like to touch them?
  How does this person use their body in relation to space?
  How does this person use the furniture in terms of support?
  How does the client move?
- *Appearance*
  How would I describe the way in which the client dresses?
  What is my impression of their level of self-care?
  How would I describe their features and what features stand out for me? (Rigid jaw, dancing hands, frozen expression, etc.).

During the course of therapy, if appropriate, we may wish to construct experiments with a view to exploring the client's 'invisible' contact functions of taste and smell, although the latter may become more 'visible' as the therapy progresses. One client complained when I burnt grapefruit oil in my therapy room, another appreciated the smell of the flowers.

Although the above questions may suggest a scripted way of assessing the client's contact functions, impressions will surface in relation to your client that have not been covered in this brief resume – I would welcome you breaking from any perceived script! What we need to be attentive to however, is that our questions have a *phenomenological* basis (see Part 3.2), that is that they facilitate description with primarily a 'how' and 'what' orientation rather than a 'why' orientation. The process of gathering information regarding your clients contact functions is part of the process of forming a fluid diagnosis upon which to base treatment planning and therapeutic strategies.

Let us not forget though that gestalt therapy is a two-way dialogue and that your client is likely to be assessing the effectiveness of your contact functions too. In one form or another the client is likely to be asking themselves similar questions as the therapist and if they are not asking themselves such questions that is information in itself.

Before you move on from this point you may wish to experiment by running through the questions listed above with a partner. As you do so remain open to other questions surfacing about the way in which each of you make and break contact.

35

The client's awareness (three zones of awareness)

Fritz Perls (1969) identified three zones of awareness:

1. Inner Zone – Concerned with internal phenomena such as feelings, emotions, dream world and bodily sensations.
2. Outer Zone – Where we make contact with our outer world through our contact functions. This is concerned with our perception of our world and the behaviours and actions we move into.
3. Middle Zone – This includes our cognitive processes, our memories, imaginings, fantasies and daydreams.

The middle mode at best integrates/moderates between inner and outer zones of awareness but it can also function in a controlling and limiting way and serve to avoid updating creative adjustments, keeping fixed gestalts in place.

You may recall the I see . . . I feel . . . I imagine . . . exercise I introduced earlier (Point 5), each of these areas relates to one of the three zones of awareness. By being attentive to each of these areas we can heighten our awareness and increase our ability to attune to our current environment and the way in which we creatively adjust to our environment. Consequently, we can improve our relationship with our perceived world. In healthy functioning there is usually rapid shuttling between all three zones of awareness with the middle zone functioning to facilitate awareness of *what is*.

As stated previously awareness is a prerequisite for full and vibrant contact with the environment. In order for the gestalt therapist to be able to work optimally she needs to be aware of how she functions in each of the three awareness zones. In moving fluidly between these zones there is an 'aggressive destructiveness and re-constructiveness' (PHG, 1951: 67) as one moves from one awareness to another. The birth of a new awareness brings about the death of the previous awareness – such is the nature of healthy gestalt formation that emerging figures are destined for destruction. It is through this on-going process of formation and destruction that we maintain contact with *what is*, rather than remain with what was, by freeing our foreground for the next relevant gestalt to emerge from our background.

The client's awareness can be diminished, numbed, automatic, blocked, moderated or interrupted (as can the therapist's). But we are not on a crusade for ever-increasing awareness without consideration for the client's situation. There are many circumstances where a dulling of awareness will serve the client well, but if such a process is incongruent with the client's current situation it could at best be limiting and at worst be life-threatening.

Tanya suffered an abusive childhood and survived her abuse creatively by desensitizing and retroflecting to protect herself through armouring and minimizing contact with her toxic environment. Her ability to make such creative adjustments is still useful today. She works for the emergency services and when faced with horrifying scenarios she has the ability to move into 'coping mode' when she just does what is needed in the crisis. However, there are times in her home life when she distances herself from her caring husband, particularly around intimacy. Alarmingly there have been occasions when she has seemingly desensitized herself from the dangers in her current environment when walking home alone late at night.

Contact is marked by excitement when that contact is sufficiently supported by the environment. When the person *feels* unsupported it leads to anxiety/fear that needs to be managed by moderating contact. The key is heightening the client's awareness of the supports that are now available; otherwise outdated, field-incongruent moderations to contact may persist.

We should not confuse meaningful awareness with an internally focused introspection that some may mistakenly consider self-awareness, but is in fact more akin to egotism. Meaningful awareness is awareness of self in relation at the contact boundary. If open to the novelty implicit in that meeting new gestalts are born, integrating past disparate awareness. 'Reality is nothing but the sum of all awareness as you experience it here and now' (F. Perls, 1969).

36

Transference, counter-transference and co-transference possibilities

Traditionally transference describes a process where the client projects a quality, trait or whole person from their past onto the therapist, 'reality' is then seen as being distorted by the client. If the therapist then identifies with this projected material and responds from this identification, this is described as their counter-transference. In traditional psychoanalysis the analyst's counter-transference was viewed negatively, or even something to be ashamed of (Sapriel, 1998).

The process of projection is key in transference and the line drawn between what is projection and what is transference is somewhat arbitrary. Generally, transference is spoken of when a whole person or blanket sets of qualities are projected onto the other, whereas projection may be referred to when a single trait is attributed to the other. The process itself is the same, 'You are putting your own attitude into the other person and then saying that this person *makes* you feel thus' (PHG, 1951: 101, original italics). PHG go on to say that it may be true that it is the other's unaware or aware intention to produce this reaction in you. This suggests that there is a passive receiver of the transference and an active projector and does not illustrate the *co-created* nature of the phenomena.

One of the potential problems with a transference/counter-transference map is that the therapist's counter-transference can simply be put down to the client's transference, absolving the therapist of responsibility. It is not then a giant leap to believing that we hold some privileged position regarding defining reality. We might consider what such a relational stance could repeat from the client's past! Transference and counter-transference are multi-directional, neither just travels from the client to the therapist or vice versa, nor does therapy take place within a bubble. The therapist is just as capable of projecting material from their past onto the client. Furthermore, from gestalt's field perspective it would be a gross mistake to view these occurrences as isolated events. Transference is not completely formed and thrown out by one party to 'land' on the other – it is created in relationship. This is why it is more accurate to use the term *co-transference* in gestalt as this, 'reflects the reality that meaning is co-created by both subjectivities, equally . . . with neither person holding a more objectively "true" version of reality in the room' (Sapriel, 1998: 42). If we fail to consider how we contribute to the way in which the client perceives us, we deprive the therapy situation of one of its most powerful and potentially healing elements.

If as Merleau-Ponty (1962) asserts, the lived present holds a past and a future within it, then characters and experiences from our past and anticipations or projections into our future will enter our present experience. Let me give an example from my practice:

My new client sat facing me hoping that I was a miracle worker, the father she never had who could take away her hurt. In my anxiety to please I attempted to meet these impossible unspoken expectations. My anxiety clouded my awareness of the process between us as I continued to try to 'rescue' this woman over the passing weeks. We got stuck and in the emerging *co-transference* my client felt hurt and disappointed, just as she had in relation to her absent father. In supervision I realized my part in this and subsequently apologized to her for having missed her and let her down. It was a tearful session, no one had ever apologized to her before – they had always blamed her.

Accepting that transference is a co-created phenomenon, it may present in any of the following forms:

1. An alienated aspect of the individual is projected onto the other (usually referred to as projection).
2. Desired hopes or yearnings are projected – an idealized mother/father/sexual partner, etc.
3. As aspects of the person's past. An affective aspect of the relationship is projected onto the current relationship, resulting in the client expecting you to treat them as they were treated historically.
4. A response to introjected beliefs, assumptions or attitudes, e.g. 'All men are bastards', 'If I'm not sexual I am worthless'.

Transference is an organizing activity in which the client assimilates the therapy situation into the thematic structures of their lifespace. The transference can be seen as a snapshot of the client's psychological relationship with the world and therefore when it arises offers the opportunity for a transformative experience. The there and then presenting in the here and now provides an opportunity of at least partial reparation of past hurts.

Experiential exercise:
Take a few moments to consider what sort of transferential reactions you might attract as a therapist. Whilst every meeting is unique there is likely to be a pattern to the way in which you relate that will lend itself to being seen in particular ways. Here are some questions that may help you – How do others generally perceive you? What roles do you have? How would you describe your sexuality? What sort of transference might best fit your age? I would also suggest that you gain feedback from others – after all, transference is a relational process!

37

How the client 'bodies forth'

We carry the history of our relationships in our bodies. As layer upon layer of creative adjustments are updated or remain outdated, the patterns we form in our relating to our world unfold. As long as we are a living body, we will body forth in the world in the way we hold ourselves, the way we move, the way we walk, and the way we make physical contact with others and the world. In doing so our histories of our contacts with the world show themselves. Our bodies forever carry information that cannot be verbalized and the way in which we body forth is a record of our on-going dialogue with the world. It is the way in which I reach out to the world, a movement in relation to my situation that defines my relationship with that situation. As person and environment are parts of a single system, 'Each participates in the creation of the other' (Beaumont, 1993). Person and environment define one another in relationship and as they define one another the degree of bodying forth and the style of that bodying forth will form.

Creative adjustment is not just a case of bodying forth; the creative adjustment can be a 'bodying back'. A disabled person can only achieve ordered behaviour through shrinkage of their environment in proportion to their disability (Goldstein, 1939). Someone with a physical disability will reorganize the proximity of her physical environment just as a person with a psychological problem reduces the size of his phenomenal world. 'What looks like a mental disturbance is in fact *an attempt to reorganize an impaired person-world relationship*' (Wollants, 2008: 66, original italics).

To illustrate possible styles of bodying forth, let us consider *possible* presentations in relation to some of the moderations to contact discussed in Part 1.

In Table 2.1 there are just a few over-simplified possibilities designed to give a flavour of a person's style of bodying forth, which will always be influenced by their situation. In the therapy

Table 2.1 **Point 37: How the Client 'Bodies Forth'**

A person who moderates contact through . . .	*May body forth by . . .*
Introjection	Gulping down the environment. Swallowing as they receive information. Have little awareness of their body. Have eyes that just want to take in.
Retroflection	Armouring their body. Present with a hardened exterior. Breathe shallowly. Walk and hold their body with muscular tightness. Have a 'hardened' way of looking.
Projection	Throw their arms out as they speak. Stick their chest out. Throw their legs out as they walk, put feet down firmly. Breathe out strongly but in quietly. Appear to look through you rather than at you.
Confluence	Eyes bulging as if person wants to merge. Bodily appear 'soft'. Collapse into their environment, e.g. 'flop' into a chair. Walk with minimal resistance.
Deflection	Fidget and be easily distracted. Breathe in short quick breaths. Move around quickly. Only engage fleetingly in eye contact.

situation, the therapist's style of bodying forth, as a figural element of the field, will impact the client's bodily movements. For example, if the therapist is confident and dramatic in their movements it begs the question where is the space for the client's confident and dramatic movements?

Kepner (1987) discussed the body processes of *overbounding* and *underbounding*. In response to an introjected belief the individual may creatively adjust by either:

Underbounding – burying their own needs and presenting as compliant so that they do not clash with the introject present in the environment. In this case the person is likely to be overly permeable in contact with others.

Overbounding – closing or hardening their contact boundary to anything that is novel or protecting themselves by attacking. The process is designed to protect through distancing from contact with the environment.

The creation of an embodied field is essential to the work of body-oriented therapy; supporting the client's development of their own embodiment; making connections between their body process and their self-experience; and using body-oriented methodology for effecting psychotherapeutic change all requires such a field. Such an approach challenges current social trends in which virtual contact can replace actual contact and medication can be used to quell or lift unpleasant emotions without consideration for their meaning.

38

Treatment planning: planning the journey

Formulating a treatment plan follows on from the process of assessment and diagnosis. As with diagnosis, treatment planning does not sit easily with many gestalt therapists probably because of prescriptive connotations. However, just as diagnosis is process diagnosis, treatment planning in gestalt considers the process of the therapy rather than prescribing a formulaic action. A gestalt therapist does not impose a treatment plan upon a client; rather the journey ahead needs to be mapped out in dialogue with the client. As with any map we need to appreciate that future twists and turns on the client's therapeutic journey will require a re-evaluation of the proposed route in response to changing goals and/or field conditions. A particular therapeutic stance may be indicated earlier in therapy that may later need adapting to facilitate on-going growth. For example, some clients may not welcome much presence from the therapist initially, but as the therapeutic relationship becomes established this could become a growing edge for the client and their relationships outside the therapy room.

The present does not exclude remembering or planning. We need to plan our therapy sessions. The therapist and the client would not arrive in the room together without mapping out a future plan! We also need to consider the wider field when delivering therapy. Therapy in many areas such as within the British National Health Service or through that delivered via insurance companies is time limited. This is a field condition. It would be irresponsible to proceed without acknowledging the limitations imposed by the structure in which the therapy takes place.

Acknowledging and addressing risk issues, together with an awareness of strategies of intervention for working with different presentations of risk, is an area of particular importance (see Point 89). A treatment plan formed in collaboration with a client to address their unique experience of the area of risk can provide a holding that greatly minimizes that risk. I talk openly with clients who have ideas of self-harm and/or suicide about those ideas.

Most experience relief in my phenomenological exploration of this desire, which then frees us to look at the 'part' of them that does not wish to self-harm or kill themselves. It also sows the seeds for possible future experimentation around this dichotomy.

In making treatment planning a collaborative venture it is imperative that the therapist considers, as far as possible, his or her own cultural influences and prejudices that colour the way in which they use diagnosis upon which treatment plans are based and the therapeutic process is conceptualized. Client and therapist could be standing upon different cultural ground. Whilst difference is often stimulating, fundamental misunderstandings about the cultural ground of another can be hurtful and shaming.

Treatment plans are formed in relation to theoretical maps and notions. It is, I believe, an ethical duty for a gestalt therapist to keep abreast of recent research in the field to update their knowledge regarding different theoretical viewpoints as they develop and review their therapeutic philosophy.

So far I have discussed treatment planning at a macro level, which we can think of as an over-arching approach for addressing potential issues and a flexible general direction for the therapy. However, a form of treatment planning takes place at a micro-level within a single session or in a brief succession of moments in a session. An example: a gestalt therapist notices her client biting his lip, breathing shallowly and hitting his own arm as he talks about his abusive father (assessment). The therapist forms a hypothesis that the client may be retroflecting anger (diagnosis). She wonders if he might benefit from experimenting with some catharsis and suggests an expressive experiment (treatment planning). An agreement to spend a session on a particular area, such as working with a dream, could also be described in such terms.

Part 3

THE THERAPY JOURNEY

Exploring the client's 'lifespace', field or situation

39

The lifespace and the field

Gestalt therapy integrated Kurt Lewin's theory of the organism–environmental field, also known as the lifespace, into its approach. His theory, central to contemporary gestalt therapy, contends that behaviour is a function of the person and the environment together, which he showed in the equation $B = f (P, E)$[8]. Lewin saw behaviour as 'being embedded in a *context* which intrinsically includes the person, with all their characteristics and perceptions, *and* the environment with all its forces and influences' (Kepner, 2003: 8, original italics).

Lewin (1952) stated that the person and the environment have to be considered as one constellation of independent factors. He called the totality of these factors the lifespace of the individual. As gestalt therapy is committed to this worldview it follows that the field with which the therapist must deal with is the lifespace of the client. The person and the psychological environment constitute that lifespace, as it exists for that person at that time in the here and now – neither can be viewed in isolation.

At this point it might be timely to note that in gestalt therapy the terms 'field', 'situation' and 'lifespace' have been used interchangeably, indeed Lewin did so himself. This has contributed to some confusion exacerbated by the term 'field' having multiple meanings and being used indiscriminately (Staemmler, 2006). There is no field per se that is perceived by one and all. In our habitually deflective language, when we talk about *the* field or *the* situation, we talk of a realm that exists outside of our lifespace, beyond our perception. For clarity we should identify who perceives the phenomena in *the* field, hence, an accurate description would be *my phenomenal* field or *my* situation. Without an engaged subjectivity as a co-constitutive pole there is no field,

---

[8] In this equation B = behaviour, f = function, P = Person, E = Environment.

fields cannot be spoken of properly as existing in themselves (McConville, 2001a).

Marrow (1969: 39) represents the lifespace diagrammatically, in the example below E = environment, P = person:

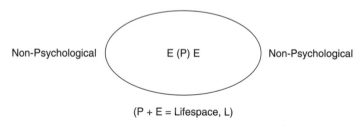

(P + E = Lifespace, L)

Figure 3.1

In Figure 3.1 the person's phenomenal world is represented within the oval and it is in the relationship between the person and the environment, within their lifespace, that the individual defines their reality. The 'non-psychological', what we may think of philosophically as a 'real' external world is unknowable. We live in an inter-subjective world. If we accept Lewin's theory it follows that to understand our clients we need to be open to their subjective perception of their environment within their lifespace – of which we become a part and influence. In Figure 3.1 the contact boundary (see Point 12) is represented by the parentheses containing (P).

Whilst acknowledging the double-edged potential for use and abuse in using the many maps available to us in gestalt therapy, Parlett (1991: 69–81) built upon and integrated the work of Lewin in recasting field theory into five principles. He identified these interrelated aspects of a field theoretical approach as:

1. The Principle of Organization – Everything is interconnected, the meaning of any singular aspect can only be derived from looking at the total situation.
2. The Principle of Contemporaneity – It is the constellation of influences in the present field that 'explains' the current behaviour. We are concerned with the field conditions at this present time not the events of the past or future.

3. The Principle of Singularity – Every person–situation field (lifespace) is unique. The individual will construct meaning and any generalizations are suspect.
4. The Principle of Changing Process – The field is in a constant state of flux, nothing is fixed. Consequently, we need to be wary of a tendency to categorize.
5. The Principle of Possible Relevance – Every part of the field impacts on the field and therefore no part of the field can be excluded in advance as irrelevant. All parts are potentially as meaningful as each other.

None of the above five principles can be applied in isolation as all are interdependent.

To believe in and follow the principles of field theory, to view the whole situation and to embrace the lifespace is not easy. To do so requires a whole paradigm shift away from an atomized and individualistic worldview towards a much wider contextual worldview. However, such a shift is needed in order to practise gestalt therapy.

> To understand the dynamics of a process, we have to comprehend the entirety of the situation involved, along with all its elements and characteristics.
>
> (Lewin, 1935: 31)

40

Viewing the lifespace through a developmental lens

A criticism often levelled at gestalt therapy is that the approach does not have a thorough enough developmental theory[9]. I believe that gestalt's rebellion against psychoanalysis's exploration of the archaic led to a de-emphasizing of the developmental theory already contained within our therapeutic philosophy[10]. Developmental theory is implicitly contained within field theory and the lifespace.

I have discussed the developmental significance Perls attached to the infant cutting teeth (Point 16). He later considered healthy development as being the transition from environmental support to self-support (F. Perls, 1973). This is inconsistent with gestalt's situational view of self. Laura Perls' (1992) stance differed markedly in seeing development as only being possible when there was adequate support available. Development through a gestalt lens of support is not a relentless march towards the individual's standing on their own two feet; this is but one pole of a support continuum. It may be a pole that in general terms we tend to move towards as we become increasingly more capable of independence in relation to our expanding experienced world. However, a process of individuating takes place within an interactional field of relations. From a field perspective development is an on-going process that is created between the individual and their environment not in the individual in isolation – developmental potential is not achieved within our own skin.

The field or situation with which the gestalt therapist deals

---

[9] There have been some fine importations into gestalt, in particular the work of Daniel Stern (1998) whose developmental theories integrate well with a gestalt view of self as process.

[10] I would like to direct the interested reader towards the work of contemporary gestalt therapists Frank (2001), Philippson (2009) and Wollants (2008).

is the lifespace of the client as perceived by that client at that moment in time. Creative adjustment through reorganizing one's response in relation to changes in the person's lifespace is central to a gestalt view of development. The person creatively adjusts in relation to their situation and their situation adjusts in relation to the individual. From a gestalt perspective development is not a series of steps leading to 'maturity'. The lifespace of a child given sufficient psychological and physical nourishment will continue to grow. Starved of physical and psychological nourishment that development will be restricted, although the child may *develop* creative adjustments in forming an imaginative 'internal' world. Similarly, the lifespace of an elderly person shrinks in many ways, but within this shrinkage there is often an on-going growth in terms of the way in which they creatively adjust to their smaller physical world.

From a field perspective my world cannot exist without me and I cannot exist without my world. Lewin discussed *existence, interdependence and contemporaneity* as attributes of an individual's lifespace.[11]

Existence – The lifespace consists of all elements that have existence for the individual: cultural, physical, biological, social, religious, familial. All impact the individual's relating and development within their world. It will also include those influences that are not present in the person's immediate field but can have a profound impact upon it. For example, the recent collapse of the banks that led to recession.

Interdependence – All elements of the field affect all other elements of the field. For a person to develop healthily is dependent upon favourable field conditions – a reasonable upbringing, encouragement from peers, a culture that allows expression of creativity. 'A person emerges from situations' (Wollants, 2008: 41).

Contemporaneity – Any behaviour depends on how the individual views the psychological situation at that moment. In gestalt we believe that present experiences and the way in which we

---

[11] I am grateful to my colleague and gestalt therapist from Australia, Sally Brookes, for sharing her thinking regarding these attributes of the lifespace.

constellate our current field emerges from our background. Our history shapes our current lifespace and can only be explored in the present through noting how an individual configures their world in the here and now. An example might be a woman who has experienced abuse from men during her upbringing then configuring her relationships with men in adulthood by keeping them at a relational distance. However, in gestalt we do not believe that we can take one aspect of the field and say that x leads to y. In the given example there will be multiple factors influencing the situation that could lead to a very different constellation of the woman's field.

You may be wondering why I have included *contemporaneity* in a section discussing the lifespace through a developmental lens. Quite simply, through the very action of you reading this page you are continuing to develop contemporaneously – in the here and now. Development has a past but it also has a present and a future.

41

The therapy space as present situation

To see a world in a grain of sand,
And heaven in a wild flower,
Hold infinity in the palm of your hand,
And eternity in an hour.

(William Blake, Auguries of Innocence, 1977)

Clients arrive for therapy not with problems *in* themselves but problems *with* their situation. They present these problems in their relating to the world in the present situation – the therapy space. As they do so the nature of these problems unfolds in the style and manner the client makes and breaks contact in the here and now of the therapy session. The way in which the client relates in the therapy situation will have shades of varying depth and colour to the way in which they constellate their world of relations outside the therapy situation. Although every meeting in every situation and every therapy session is unique, there are patterns of relating in all of us that will play out across situations. We may call this character, style or personality – it is an essential part of who we are. However, this can lead to rigidity and loss of a healthy fluidity in relating. The style that developed in the past plays out in the present.

I see many areas worthy of consideration as I sit facing a fellow human being experiencing discord in their situation. How can I make sense of the way the client makes and breaks contact? How does this relate to their perceived malfunctioning field of relationships? How does this person affect me and can I make any sense of my reaction in relation to what is presented? The possibilities may be endless, but the answers and choices of direction lie on the surface if we only pay attention to what the client is telling us in all the ways in which they communicate. Our reactions to their way of being with us and theirs to us give us all the raw data we need, and will be evident from the first moment we meet in the way in which we body forth to one another.

I have been struggling in trying to convey this aspect of field theory. The mists of my confusion are now lifting as I make sense of my struggle to explain my thinking regarding the therapy space as the present situation. I believe that my struggle reflects a confusion that arises in others when trying to gain an understanding of field theory. The field of any one person holds an infinite number of possibilities. Yet we can only deal with the most figural possibilities in the present situation – and here I am attempting to cover all possible eventualities! Just as I get stuck here, stuckness, or impasse, is a common feature of therapy (and life). Whilst the therapist may be able to facilitate movement through interventions, there is no guarantee that these will provide insight or awareness and there is often a need to remain with impasse.

> For the purposes of therapy only the present structure of the person-world interaction is available.
>
> (PHG 1951: 61)

The present situation contains more than the client and the therapist and more than their collective histories. Many settings that we encounter seem to meet us with a will of their own and challenge us to act in certain ways – fields dialogue with us. Such a dynamic is true for the therapy space as much as any other space. For a client new to therapy, the field may be speaking in a foreign language. The field in which the therapy takes place will have its own 'voice' and what it 'says' will depend upon, amongst other factors, the history of the person it is speaking to, the relational stance of the therapist and the location of the therapy.

When we meet with clients we need to gain an understanding of how they organize their field and what is causing them to constellate their field in this way.

Case example

A client has been a victim of a road traffic accident in which a white transit van ran into the side of him. His children were in the car at the time and he could do nothing to avoid the collision. Since the accident he has become oversensitized to possible dangers on the roads due to an overwhelming need to ensure his family and he himself remain safe. In response to his need for safety he is constantly anxious and alert to any possible dangers. He is hyper-vigilant when he sees any white transit van, which triggers particularly strong memories of his accident. He begins to recall past events where his safety was threatened, resulting in a greater need for certainty and security, exacerbated by his projecting into the future about what dangers could befall his children. He attempts to minimize uncertainty by avoiding driving at busy times or on busy roads before withdrawing from driving completely. He continues to organize his field around his need for safety, security and certainty through avoidance.

As we say in gestalt, one thing leads to another. A need organizes the field, the field talks back and a new need forms and so the process continues. The only certainty we have is that there will be constant change. Although the need organizes the field and we need an understanding of the person's need, it would be a mistake to attempt to study that need in isolation. Many links have been made between findings in quantum physics that show that we cannot study one specific thing in isolation (Philippson, 2009), as there is no specific isolated thing in existence. There are only interrelated fields of energy and these principles support gestalt's field perspective.

43

Investigating supports

Lewin's field (or situation) is only ever a field of a certain person at a certain time in a certain place. It follows from a field perspective that what is supportive for the person in one situation does not necessarily transport to being supportive in another situation. At a micro level a teacher returning from work may or may not feel supported at the sight of her three-year-old son depending upon the constellation of her field at that moment. If preoccupied with the lesson for the following day's assessment, she may feel very differently to a situation where she has just had a successful day and school holidays have commenced. At a macro level certain cultures will be more supportive of an embodied way of being whilst others will support a more cognitive way of being. In defining support Lee and Wheeler (1996) asked what kinds of connection/disconnection lead to rich figure formation with the possibilities for increased interconnection within the situation.

Experiential exercise
Draw a map of your supports including all types of relationships: interpersonal, hobbies, interests, activities, challenges, withdrawal and any other supports that may apply for you. Now consider in what circumstances each of these potential supports moves into being less supportive or a pressure, for example, the need to keep up with friends may become a burden at times. Then consider what best supports you physically: nourishing healthy food, firm ground to stand upon, furniture that is supportive, exercise, sufficient sleep, warmth, a healthy and inspiring environment. Can you build upon your supports?

As therapists we need to be sufficiently supported ourselves in order to be able to truly support our clients (see Point 95). We need a healthy work–life balance, if we support ourselves well we will be better equipped to support our clients. If we are consistently under-supported in our lives and work then our clients pick up on this on-going field event.

Support and connection are vital components in any healing process. Persistent disconnection due to a lack of support for contact can lead to various forms of physical and psychological dis-ease. As we shall see in the following point, reactions such as guilt and shame are maintained through a disconnection with the current field and a connection with an archaic isolating field in which there was a lack of support.

In the past gestalt has been guilty of failing to build sufficient relational ground to support challenge or catharsis.[12] Such *figure therapy* looked impressive and dramatic, but without sufficient ground-support meaningful change does not take place. Like-wise, inadequately trained self-appointed 'gestalt therapists' have abused experiments such as the empty chair, inaccurately billing an experiment that lays on the surface of the 'therapy', as oil on water, as gestalt therapy. Therapists need to be supported in their work with a coherent theoretical philosophy to be able to support their clients ethically with care and wisdom.

Now more than at any other time in history we live in a field where we can achieve a level of gratification almost instantly. Speed seems to be of the essence from fast food to faster broad-band. We can use caffeine to keep us going, alcohol to relax us. Within such a cultural field it is not surprising that clients often arrive looking for quick remedies to presenting problems that are supported by a complex matrix of creative adjustments formed over time. Although the presenting issue may be managed, and in the short term this may be supportive, for lasting change the issues that are supporting the presenting issue need to be addressed. Addressing such sedimented ways of being cannot be done by simply thinking it through. We need to create an *embodied field*. If a client rushes into our therapy room in a dis-embodied state, the gestalt therapist might pay attention to the impact the client's way of being is having upon her bodily reactions and invite the client to do likewise.

---

[12] There is a twenty-minute video session of gestalt therapy by Fritz Perls with a client called 'Gloria' that was filmed and is still held up as an example of gestalt therapy. It is this twenty-minute film that has caused the most misconceptions and misunderstanding about the approach.

Support is a broad area and to break it down it may be useful to consider three areas: What supports the client? What supports the therapist? What supports are needed in the current situation?

44

Shame and guilt as functions of the field

Broadly speaking guilt is felt in response to an action that is felt to be wrong, shame is felt in response to a way of being that is felt to be wrong – each is marked by hiding. Simplistically we could say that guilt is when I make a mistake, shame is when I am a mistake. Both shame and guilt form in relationship but can be maintained, and deepened in isolation. They are characterized by a rupture between the individual and their field. Consequently, the person only lets in information that reinforces their self-perception of wrongness. Whilst disconnection prevents any reworking of the fixed gestalts that support unhealthy guilt and shame, the connection with its possibilities for support that have the potential to act as an antidote can hold so much fear as to virtually guarantee avoidance. One of the prime tasks for the therapist is to track the client and attune to possible guilt and shame triggers and ruptures in the therapeutic relationship.

The process of introjection plays a key role in forming and maintaining guilt and shame. Perls maintains that introjects form because of over-control by the environment. He spoke primarily of explicit messages in relation to authoritarian child rearing (Wheeler, 1991). These are not the only introjected beliefs that can guide us. At a deeper level are the unexamined attitudes and beliefs that McConville (2001) refers to as 'ground introjects'. The core of this deeper material is composed of learned beliefs that a behaviour, felt need or part of the person's way of being is unacceptable in the field. If this deep belief concerns behaviour it will probably support guilt, for example, if masturbation is considered bad, wrong or even evil in the person's field. If this deeper level of introjection relates to the person's felt need or way of being they are likely to experience shame. However, in this simplified hypothesis I am not saying that it is a case of either/or; we can experience guilt and shame.

A ground introject that a part of the person is unacceptable in their field is not simply swallowed whole, but is taken in from their environment through a process more akin to osmosis. In a grossly shaming or guilt-ridden upbringing, the person breathes in their wrongness in every moment of their infancy.

'People live and grow in the context of relationship' (PHG, 1951). Regarding shame, people also shrivel and shrink in the context of pathological relationship. Behaviours that are unacceptable in the individual's formative field can result in guilt and shame-binds in relation to 'forbidden' behaviours or needs. For example, a parent pulls away from a child when the child cries for nurturance and continues to do so repeatedly. To make the environment safe the infant makes a necessary creative adjustment by making a part of itself wrong. To do otherwise would risk abandonment, a consequence being the formation of a distress–shame bind. The child's belief that their distress is dangerous to relationship may be carried for life. Although I illustrate a distress–shame bind, this is but one example of a shame bind – choose your need and that can develop into a shame bind. It is often *needs* in particular that lead to shame and shame binds. This suggests to me that such shame binds are more prevalent in an individualistic culture where dependence is less acceptable. In a field that does not support the need, the person loses a voice for it. Whenever the shame-linked need arises, the person experiences shame to enable them to live in some sort of harmony within their lifespace.

Shame, and to a lesser extent guilt, are major regulators of the boundary between self and other. In the act of contact between self and other, the self-boundary is continually redefined (Lee, 1995). In order to grow healthily one must receive enough support from the field. Guilt and shame indicate a rupture between the individual's needs and the environmental receptivity to meet those needs. There is a breakdown in the process of organizing the field into 'self' and 'other'. Resolution can be accomplished through confusion over the self–other boundary, the unacceptable need being disowned and made 'not me'.

These affects are not unilaterally unhealthy, without them we would engage in any behaviour to satisfy any need where control is needed. Sociopathic behaviour results from a lack of such affects. Guilt and shame both involve the process of retroflection. For example, shame in its simplest form of shyness or embarrassment can be seen as a natural process of retroflection that guards our privacy. Shame is continually useful in our daily lives. It enables the person to pull back when there is no immediate support. It tells us when our interest is not being received so that we may reframe our interest (Lee, 1995).

42

The need organizes the field

A hiker has been on a challenging walk acutely aware of his empty water bottle, a constant reminder of his thirst. He happens upon a rushing freshwater river and with relief gulps down some of the fast-flowing water. On the opposite bank a fisherman is casting his fly and watching the river intently for the possible bite of a salmon. An ecologist is measuring the depth and flow of the river to assess whether the water level has dropped and the feasibility of harnessing its energy, whilst a canoeist rushes by on those same currents. Two young children splash playfully in the shallows of the riverbank, watched by their mother grateful for a few minutes respite from their energetic demands. The same river perceived in radically different ways according to the person's needs.

Lewin (1938) considered that we create a map of our landscape based upon our need at that moment in time. He gave an example, similar to the one above, of a soldier in wartime and a farmer in peacetime viewing the same field of corn based on their needs. People are always actively organizing their fields. They do so in relation to their current needs which will be influenced by past experience. For example, our hiker may have had an experience of poisoning from drinking from a river and choose to remain thirsty, or the mother may not allow herself to enjoy the experience of space from her children through an introjected belief that this would be neglectful and make her a bad mother.

Self-awareness is often spoken of as an internal event disconnected from others. In gestalt self-awareness is a field event – strictly speaking it is self-as-process-awareness. Any of the individuals in my given example, if self-aware, would be aware of the figural aspects of their *phenomenal field* impacting upon their functioning in the here and now. Their behaviour will be influenced by their past and their anticipated future, but it will be the present dynamics of the current field (of which past and future are a part) in which the figural need surfaces that will influence the behaviour and organize the field.

45

A setting for challenge and experiment

Lydia, a successful businesswoman, arrived for her initial therapy session with me with a forceful air. She strode into the room and perched herself firmly on the edge of the sofa, her erect posture accentuated by her pinstriped suit. She told me that she'd been in therapy before and had a working knowledge of different modalities. 'So tell me, what led you to consider therapy with a gestalt therapist?' I inquired. Her response was rapid, 'I want to be challenged!' To her surprise I invited her to lean back into the sofa, to feel her arm being supported, movements that she struggled to make. As she sat there stiffly resisting the support from the furniture I made a further inquiry, 'And what might be a challenge for you?' She smiled over a trembling bottom lip as her eyes began to water.

Part of the art of therapy is to push at the client's growing edge sufficiently to facilitate change whilst being respectful of their struggle and the ground from which their difficulties arise. As I have illustrated above, challenging a client does not necessarily mean vigorous confrontation or the client 'getting into' some strong emotion. Any experiment needs to emerge in the relationship in an environment that is sufficiently holding. By building a supportive ground through respectful dialogue in which we appreciate the client's situation and their perception of it, we create the conditions in which we can push at the client's growing edge. This groundwork is key to the creation of the *safe emergency* where sufficient support is built to hold the client as they move into unfamiliar territory.

A gestalt field perspective informs us that the landscapes we co-create in relation to our environment form our sense of self. It is through the lens of these experiences that we view any new experience. In healthy functioning we will use this new experience to question and reassess our original map. Carefully graded experimentation and challenge in therapy, the creation of the *safe emergency*, can facilitate such questioning and lead to fundamental change through revising outdated modes of self-perception. Through experimentation we can vividly bring alive past experience to re-assess the usefulness of behaviours in the current field. In essence we re-evaluate our *narrative self*, the story we tell ourselves about who we are in the world made up from the creative adjustments made to this point in our life.

Fixed gestalts may have been the only supports available for the client in an otherwise barren landscape. Such beliefs will have been valued allies and one cannot necessarily just talk a client out of such embodied beliefs even if they are well past their sell-by date. By carefully constructing experiments *with* the client, the fixed gestalt that formed experientially can be dismantled experientially, thereby freeing space for the formation of a new experience and constructed reality. The challenge for the client and the therapist is to create a situation that will facilitate experimentation that challenges fixed and outdated ways of being and leads to such metamorphosis.

Whilst movement away from the familiar can be exciting, it can often be uncomfortable, feel threatening or it can even feel as though one's world will collapse. Consequently, movement away from what Polster and Polster (1973) termed the *familiarity boundary* can result in the contact boundary becoming hardened and impermeable, as the person becomes resistant to change, limiting themselves to life-restricting familiar situations. 'I-am-what-I-am gets hardened into I-am-what-I-have-always-been-and always-will-be' (ibid: 119). For such people changes in their environment can feel catastrophic due to their prior behaviour of minimizing the unfamiliar. For change to take place there needs to be a moment where the client lets go of the familiar and enters the *void*. There are a series of moments when the skydiver leaps from the aeroplane and hurtles towards the ground not knowing whether his parachute will open. Staying with the void holds similar uncertainty.

46

The cultural field

Experiential exercise
Imagine that you are sitting in your therapy room which you have
decorated and furnished to your choice. Take a few moments to
consider the contents of the room. Now picture yourself sitting with
a client. What stands out for you as you picture this client? What are
they wearing?

I would now like to take the liberty of making a few assumptions. I imagine that at least 95% of the people reading this book
are white. I imagine that the vast majority of you thought of a
white client. I also imagine that the way in which you visualized
your therapy room reflected your cultural background. Culture is,
of course, more than skin colour and soft furnishings but what I
am hoping the above exercise illustrates is that we naturally gravi-
tate towards what is culturally familiar without even realizing it.
What is culturally unfamiliar is far less accessible.

Jacobs (2000) discusses 'white skin privilege', and gestalt therapy and psychotherapy in general in the western world is white-
skin privileged.[13] According to Jacobs one of the white-skin
privileges we possess is a total lack of consciousness of it and the
privilege that accompanies it. The cost of bringing white privilege
into awareness shifts the privileged position of power we enjoy as
whites from something that just is to something that is fluid and
hence could change.

Experience is formed within a particular cultural context. I
form in process with my culture and I also shape my culture. Our

---

[13] Men from African and Caribbean backgrounds have been disproportionately represented in mental health services in the UK. They
are more likely to come to the attention of services via the criminal
justice system, more likely to delay engaging with the services due to
negative perceptions and more likely to receive mandatory treatment
(Keating, 2007).

culture will shape and frame the limits of what can be communicated and expressed; it forms the ground we stand upon and the lenses through which we view our world. Consequently, meaning making is culturally contextual and, as meaning-making maps, so are psychotherapy theories.

A gestalt philosophy with its focus on phenomenology, its appreciation of the lifespace, the client's situation and the individual as part of a greater whole possesses a relational stance for appreciating cultural difference. However, like any other psychotherapy, gestalt stands upon a cultural worldview that excludes other cultural worldviews. Our ground is built upon gestalt's popularity in the West in the 1960s when seemingly everything revolved around the individual and individual responsibility at the expense of community and family (Mackewn, 1997). A consequence was that those ways of being that matched the culture at the time were seen in a more positive light than those that clashed with Anglo-American values. One such example from gestalt theory can be seen in how, historically, confluence and introjection, moderations that are about taking in from or merging with the environment, were viewed in more negative terms than those moderations that separated the person from their environment. A further example could be seen in the valuing of self-support above environmental support. A lot has changed but it seems inevitable that blind spots will exist.

My culture is embodied and as such will shape not only my thinking but also impact the way I hold my body and the way in which I use my contact functions in relation to my environment. I manipulate my environment and my environment manipulates me, cultural norms and values shape the way I hold myself. For instance, if it is not culturally acceptable to make direct eye contact, I not only look down with my eyes but this movement affects my whole body. I will then continue to hold muscle groups in this way as both comfortable and familiar. Such cultural norms will occur out of awareness.

Culture shapes our very perception of things. The Maoris have 3,000 names for different colours; this is not because they perceive more colours than other races but because they are unable to identify them when they belong to objects that are structurally different. Language is culturally embodied. Two people from the same culture share a more intimate understanding of their language and its meaning than the most fluent of foreigners. We shape the words we form and the words we form shape us. The way in which we hold our jaw will be shaped as much by our language as the way in which a Muslim woman holds her posture in public places.

47

Creative experimentation

An experiment needs to emerge from the dialogue as a phenomenological exploration of the client's field of relations. Whilst recognizing that the whole of a person's field will impact upon them, we deal with the figural aspects of the person's situation. These figural elements include the therapist's reactions whether disclosed or not. Any experiment needs to be created in relation to these figural elements but the therapist needs to remain open to changes in focus and direction. In suggesting an experiment and moving into it we take a step without knowing what the next step will be; if we format the experiment it ceases to become a creative experiment and moves into some form of prescribed behaviour modification.

The gestalt experiment is designed to venture beyond the client's familiarity boundary, to break from habitual ways of being by creating a safe emergency where the client can explore different ways of being. It is designed to heighten the client's awareness of their current existence and how their present experience might be shaped by their past experience. As such it is the cornerstone of experiential learning. The limits of creative experimentation are decided in the therapeutic relationship between client and therapist and are shaped by existing field conditions including moral and ethical boundaries.

The gestalt experiment is underpinned by the belief that we learn at a deeper level and in a more embodied way experientially. Such learning might include taking what appear to be wrong turnings or blind alleys but this is all part of the process of active engagement in experimentation. An experiment is just what it says; the therapist encourages the client to play with different ways of being with the aim of heightening the client's awareness. Gestalt experiments are not solution focused but can lead to solutions. Within the holding environment of the therapy session the client can be facilitated to explore a wide range of relational dilemmas that can be brought to life through experimentation.

Sometimes the therapist will use their expertise and creativity in constructing an experiment and at other times the experiment may be constructed between client and therapist. Consensus should be reached between therapist and client and the experiment should be graded appropriately, meaning that the experiment needs to be enough of a stretch for the client without being too much of a leap. If you were learning to play the piano you would begin with practising scales and simple melodies before playing Chopin.

A well-known (and often abused) gestalt experiment is 'the empty chair'. Pioneered by Fritz Perls at a time when the psychotherapy world was engaged in 'talking about', the technique brings issues from the there and then 'out there' into the here and now of the therapy room. Commonly a character from the client's life (past or present) is imagined to be sitting in the empty chair and the client is invited to dialogue with this character using immediate present-centred language. The therapist is likely to be looking for ways in which the client disowns their power and moderates their behaviour. The empty chair technique can be used in many different ways: to explore a quality the client disowns, to represent an organization, for the client to dialogue with a split they have identified within themselves, to represent a life choice, to re-own projections, to name a few possibilities. What is critical when moving to suggest such an experiment is that the relational groundwork between client and therapist has been built sufficiently.

Although experiments can be elaborate, dramatic, cathartic and involve all sorts of 'props' from paints to sand-trays, punchbags to pillows, the success of an experiment is not measured by the volume of the expression. Successful experimentation leads to increased awareness of the client's habituated ways of being, creating the opportunity for a wider degree of choice. Some of the most effective experiments are the simplest such as encouraging a client to stay with an uncomfortable feeling, developing a small movement made by the client or encouraging them to try out a different posture.

In gestalt we do not seek the cause of events in the nature of isolated behaviour but in the relationship between behaviour and its surroundings (Lewin, 1936). We will not find 'the answer' in a single isolated creative experiment. An experiment is a useful figural exercise in gestalt therapy that will fall into the ground of the therapeutic relationship. For instance, an experiment that facilitates an expression of anger at an authority figure can lead to a reconfiguration of the client's field in relation to his expressing strong emotion. Such a change occurs in the ground as new embedded awareness sediments down, replacing past creative adjustments.

Sandra: I'm filling Sandra's head. Stuffing myself into every corner and leaving no space for her ... just like her Mum, Dad, husband, children, job – all those damned responsibilities that all fall on me! *(Energy increases.)*

It is often useful for the therapist to use metaphor too, for example in response to the above making a brief process comment such as, 'When you began you sounded like a tired old steam train, you now sound like an energized express train'.

Fantasy involves projection and is an expansive activity as it reaches beyond the client's actual situation. The client's ability to fantasize may manifest in the form of catastrophic fantasies. This is not necessarily something to shy away from; a clinical choice can be to follow through the fantasy to a conclusion. For example, a client says she is fearful of asking her partner to help her more around the house. The therapist asks what might happen if she did and her fantasy is that he may end up deserting her. The process of inquiry continues along 'and what might happen then' lines, revealing the clients underlying fantasized fears. The movement can then be made to exploring the likelihood of these fears being realized, the meaning of them and how this fear is supported in her field. From a process point of view the client's ability to catastrophize displays their creative ability to project into the future. Simply noticing this as ability, rather than investing in moving away from the negative focus can facilitate a movement into other forms of engaging with fantasy.

Areas involving fantasy that can serve to bring figural elements of the client's wider field into the therapy room include contact with: a resisted event, a resisted feeling, a resisted personal trait, facing a 'real' or imagined situation (as above), an inaccessible person or organization, resolving unfinished business, exploring unfamiliar aspects of oneself, exploring/imagining the unknown.[14]

One of my colleagues who works with clients experiencing sexual dysfunction has a favourite saying – that the most powerful

---

[14] For the interested reader Polster and Polster (1973) discuss some of these areas in more depth.

sexual organ is the brain. What she means by this is our capacity to use our imagination and to fantasize. Our capacity to fantasize has immense power across all areas of our functioning and can be invested in nourishing or destroying us. We are creative beings; the choice that faces us is how we invest our creativity.

49

Homework and practising

Experimentation in gestalt therapy does not have to be limited to the therapy session. One of the aims of gestalt therapy is to expand the client's awareness continuum so that they are able to find alternative supports and fully utilize existing supports. In one sense we could say that we work to try to put ourselves out of business! The point of therapy is not for the client to have wonderful contact with the therapist exclusively in the therapy room. New relational skills and abilities that emerge from increased awareness in therapy need practice beyond the therapy space and with such practice there are pitfalls. For example, clients who have just discovered an ability to assert themselves may over-stretch into aggressive or over-assertive relating or receive a hostile response. If new ways of being are practised outside therapy the client can then re-evaluate their efforts and reactions with their therapist in the holding environment of the therapy room.

Some gestalt therapists have been surprised when in collaboration with clients I have set homework between sessions under some misguided impression that this is for the behaviourists. Experimenting with new behaviours is a key part of gestalt therapy in heightening the client's awareness. Some reasons for incorporating homework with clients are as follows:

1. They are in the situation and have probably come for therapy because of some dissatisfaction/problem with their situation.
2. If we deny use of homework and practice we are separating out a part of the person's situation and restricting opportunity.
3. Therapy might be time-limited. Utilizing time between sessions is an efficient use of time.
4. It can be an extension of an experiment completed in the session – an increase in the grading of the experiment.
5. It connects the client's life outside the therapy room with their life inside the therapy room.

6. The client has the therapist's support available should things 'go wrong' in some way.

Possible dangers if new ways of being are not 'tested out' in the client's wider situation:

-   A fixed gestalt is formed, e.g. 'I am assertive' without consideration for a wide range of possible field conditions.
-   The client withdraws in response to a perceived negative reaction from an element or elements of the field, e.g. partner critically says, 'You've changed since you saw that therapist'.
-   An artificial split between a therapy world and 'out there' is created and covertly encouraged out of awareness by the therapist.

Just as we do not suggest an experiment in the session to attain a certain result so the same principle applies with homework. An experiment is just that and although it will always lead somewhere we know not where. The homework, as with any experiment, needs to dovetail into the particular area of the client's situation that is impacting them at the time.

Focus on experience: phenomenology in gestalt therapy

48

Use of metaphor and fantasy

The use of metaphor expands our capacity to convey our felt sense verbally. Fantasy allows us to make sense of our experience by adding a narrative to that experience.

Experiential exercise
Think of an emotional experience you have had and describe that experience in literal terms. Then describe either the same experience or another with the freedom to use metaphor and fantasy. If you are doing this with a partner, ask for feedback regarding the impact it had on them and also consider the level of your engagement with your material. What helped you both connect with the material?

Rather than being solely internal creations metaphors and fantasies are created in relation with our world, even if they relate to isolation. As such they can provide valuable insights into the other's phenomenal field, but only if we resist the temptation to interpret and remain open to receiving the other's description. As we develop language our growing dependence upon verbal expression restricts our ability to convey our actual intersubjective experience (Stern, 1998). Use of metaphor can add colour, form and texture to our verbal communication and in doing so build an intersubjective bridge between I and other, retrieving at least some of what has been lost before the spoken word dominated the expression of our experience.

The starting point for an experiment can often be in reaction to a client's use of metaphor or fantasy. For example:

Therapist: *(experiences the client as distant with low energy)* What is standing out for you right now?
Sandra: My head feels like it's full of cotton wool, I wish I could just take it off.
Therapist: I've got a suggestion. Speak as if you are the cotton wool in Sandra's head.

50

Sensations and feelings

> Do not look for anything behind phenomena; they them-
> selves are the lesson.
>
> (Goethe, 1998)

Sensations are the raw data from which awareness emerges. To allow awareness to emerge we need to allow space for the full figure of the sensation to form. In a fast paced world in which virtual reality can be a substitute for feeling the wind against our faces, there are considerable forces in our fields to deny us such space. Technical advances can desensitize us from human contact with others and ourselves. In gestalt we fly in the face of much of our cultural way of being by inviting clients to stay with sensations and feelings. Sense experience is our communication with the world. A sensation or feeling does not exist in isolation but within a field of relations including other sensations and feelings. The relevance of the sensation or feeling for the individual experiencing it will depend upon where it surfaces in relation to the their situation.

The phenomenologist Merleau-Ponty (1962) saw perception as intrinsically linked to sensate experience and invited us to consider each of our senses as constituting a small world within a larger one. If we see ourselves as functioning in several small 'sense-worlds', paradoxically we will create the opportunity for connectedness and integration.

We have a felt sense of the world long before we are able to describe our experience. Stern (1998) theorizes on pre-verbal development and what is lost when the child enters what he refers to as the verbal domain of relatedness. The development of language with its limited feeling and sensing vocabulary has the effect of pre-structuring feelings and sensations in that we feel or sense what we can describe rather than attempt to describe what we feel and sense. We are restricted in putting our somatic experiences into words – the language just doesn't exist. In describing sensations and feelings we may need to step away from literal explanation, feeling words, and towards metaphor and images. The vast majority of therapies, including gestalt, have strong verbal and cognitive biases that lead to a valuing of what can be explained. Culturally it is difficult for us just to stay with a sensation or a feeling, particularly one that does not immediately lend itself to a neat category within our inadequate verbal vocabulary. So often we move on to find a cognitive understanding prematurely for what, if we only allowed ourselves the space, may sediment down into an embodied experience.

There is a danger that theories can lead us away from our immediate experience; notions such as, 'behind every anger is a hurt' (Hycner, 1993) and 'behind every depression is a rage' (Wheeler, 1991) might generally be useful clinical wisdom, but only if we hold it lightly. In gestalt we need to hold an attitude of uncertainty – *a* does not always lead to *b* even though it often does. Working phenomenologically we need to be wary of moving into an interpretive model of psychotherapy that preconfigures the field through predicting the client's unexpressed experience or believing that another experience lies beneath what we see on the surface. We need to accept what is.

Sensations can be the entry point with a client in gestalt therapy – to adapt Freud's quote,[15] they could be seen as the royal road to awareness. Gestalt therapists seek to heighten awareness of sensations trusting the client's process to use full and vibrant contact with their senses to inform them regarding their needs. Assisting a client in increasing their awareness of the meaning of their sensations could involve experimentation, such as inviting them to give a voice to a sensation and to speak from that sensation.

We live in a culture that de-emphasizes the unitary nature of human beings. In feeling our sensations and being curious about others' sensations, we help ensure that we practise gestalt as an embodied therapy rather than separating ourselves off into component parts.

---

[15] In 'The Interpretation of Dreams' Sigmund Freud (1997) referred to dreams as 'The royal road to the unconscious'.

51

Co-creation, temporality and horizontalism

From a phenomenological and field perspective, my very existence depends upon my being in contact with the world and my world being in contact with me. I touch the world and the world touches me in a dialogue that changes both my world and me.

We are all situated in the world and, in being situated, things, events and people press in upon us. The way in which I perceive my world will differ from the way any other being perceives the world; hence, we refer to my perception of my world as my *phenomenal world* or my *phenomenal field*. It is a given that we are in contact with the world, but the level of that contact will depend upon a plethora of field conditions that will directly affect our individual perception of our respective worlds. Kennedy (1998: 89) discusses three basic movements that mark being situated. These three 'movements' are: co-creation, temporality and horizontalism.

Co-creation

Our lives are a prolonged dialogue with those around us and with our phenomenal world. We need the existence of others to define ourselves. In the language of phenomenology the 'I' requires the existence of the other to enable the 'I' to have a phenomenal reality, in other words reality is co-created. 'I' needs 'other' to exist. We do not live in a void.

> . . . man is in the world and only in the world does he know himself.
>
> (Merleau-Ponty, 1962: xi)

Temporality

My experience is not something that I live through and discard, although we may often hear clients express wishes to do so through a desire to 'move on' from painful or difficult situations. I am my experience, I carry my experience in my body, and my past experience directly affects my current experience. In every moment in my life I bring the totality of my past.

Gestalt therapy's emphasis upon present experience can be misunderstood. The here and now does not stand in isolation, there is a story behind every current experience and that story, extending back to the beginning of life, shapes and moulds every current experience from the unremarkable to the bizarre. Our histories shape our expectations in the present and our dreams for the future.

> The lived present holds a past and a future within its thickness.
>
> (Merleau-Ponty, 1962: 275)

Horizontalism

In gestalt we aim to maintain a horizontal relationship with our clients rather than promote vertical relating. We acknowledge that there are real differences in the client–therapist relationship but we do not constellate the relationship as teacher–pupil or doctor–patient. We enter the relationship in the service of the between of that relationship. The therapy relationship is not equal; the client is the focus of our attention and they seek help from us for which we may get paid – there is a power imbalance. However, we have a shared humanity and in our humanity we are equals, we are all beings-in-the-world. If we use techniques to move our client towards our goal for the client, we are not practising gestalt and we are promoting vertical relating. If we act in this way we reduce the responsibility and support of the client (L. Perls, 1978), thereby diminishing the client and elevating ourselves. In a vertical relationship the therapist's reaction may remain hidden, alternatively they may self-disclose indiscriminately or with prejudice. In the horizontal relationship the therapist is willing to show herself and to be fully present with the client in the service of the dialogue.

The principles of co-creation, temporality and horizontalism need to be fully embraced in order to practise gestalt therapy.

These three principles form the foundations upon which the three pillars that are the bedrock of gestalt therapy stand. To reiterate, those three pillars are: existential phenomenology, field theory and dialogue.

52

Intentionality: reaching out and making sense of my world

> We are all beings-in-the-world in the sense that we all share
> an intentionally derived conscious experience of the world
> and ourselves, through which we make the distinctions such
> as those relating to notions of 'I' and 'not I'.
>
> (Spinelli, 1989: 26)

In phenomenology an act of intentionality is the process of
reaching out to my world and the stimuli in my world in order to
translate it into meaningful experience. Although we are all interconnected we each have our individual ways of perceiving and
making sense of our world coloured and shaped by our past. In
that sense we inhabit the same world *and* different worlds.

Intentionality was originally described as a mental phenomenon. According to the phenomenologist Edmund Husserl (1931)
an act of intentionality has two foci, *what* is experienced and *how*
it is experienced – the mode of experiencing. The former is made
up of the content of my experience and the latter how my history
and points of reference influence my process of experiencing. For
example, I look out of the window and in the street I focus on a
parked dark blue car. Meaning is added to my experience of this
unremarkable vehicle as I recall my wife's previous car of a similar colour that was very difficult to keep clean. I'm in touch with
my dislike for dark blue cars as the owner of the one I am looking
at carefully polishes his. The owner and myself are both reaching
out to an object in the world but we are each making different
sense of this object. In phenomenology the concept of intentionality implies that in any action there is a definite point of reference, a sharp figure. In my example this could be the dark blue car,
and then shift to the apparent difference in attitudes between the
owner and myself.

Merleau-Ponty did not see intentionality as solely a mental
process but considered sensations and feelings to be 'the intentional

tissue which the effort to know will take apart' (1962: 53). He viewed an act of intentionality as emergent, the person reaches out to their world and a hazy figure begins to form. This is indicative of a movement from id functioning. Perception is an active act and contained within my reaching out to make sense of my world is interpretation without which my world would simply be a confusing mass of ground phenomena, even then I would be interpreting this as confusion. We decide what is figural as we perceive and construct our experiential world as we reach out to it and our world gives itself to us – the glass of water invites drinking, the sunset invites gazing and the tearful client invites comforting or irritation.

By intentionality Husserl meant that all our thinking, feeling and acting are always about things in the world. All conscious awareness is intentional awareness; all consciousness is consciousness-of-something.

> Given the nature of an act of intentionality with its two foci of the "what" of experience and the "how" of experience it is no coincidence that in gestalt when seeking description of the client's immediate experience we do not concern ourselves with a "why" orientation, but concentrate on a "what" and "how" perspective.
>
> (Levitsky and Perls, 1970).

53

Transcendental phenomenology and Husserl

My wife and I were decorating and had just finished painting a wall. We stood back to admire our work. 'That's got a lovely subtle blue tinge', she said. 'It's not a blue tinge, it's green', I replied. We invited a neighbour round to see what she thought, 'I like the purple hue', she said. No one was wrong.

In terms of perception and experience there are as many worlds as there are people on the planet. Phenomenology and field theory take the philosophical position that if there is not a perceiver then there is not a world.

The phenomenologist Edmund Husserl (1859–1938) began as a mathematician before moving to study philosophy. He developed an interest in how humans make meaning and studied here and now experience, how things surfaced in awareness and the patterns we create from the plethora of information and perceptions that are available to us in any one moment. In doing so Husserl focused on conscious processes, but he did so from a biological stance rather than from the relational stance adopted by existential phenomenology (see Point 55).

Transcendental phenomenology is so called because Husserl believed that through engaging in a three-step process of *phenomenological reduction*, discussed in the following point, we are able to transcend assumed knowledge. Husserl saw the process of phenomenological reduction as central to his philosophy. Once our knowledge had been transcended he considered that we were then in a position to gain an objective view of the world through our senses, as opposed to making interpretations of sensory data, enabling us to gather knowledge through what he described as *original experience*. Husserl believed that knowledge begins with wonder, the sort of wonder we see in a child's eyes as they experience something for the first time. Curiosity arises from that experience of wonder around the events and this leads to the seeking of an explanation uncontaminated by previous experience.

Husserl thought that all knowledge should be based on experience. He described transcendental phenomenology as a rigorous science because it investigates the way that knowledge comes into being and clarifies the assumptions upon which all human understanding is grounded. To make meaning Husserl believed that experience needed to be consulted repeatedly.

Whilst phenomenology integrates well with field theory in that both see perception and interpretation of the world as completely unique to each individual, Husserl's transcendental phenomenology moves away from a field theoretical viewpoint in his belief that we can stand aside from our world through separating the observer from the observed. This aspect of Husserl's theory is incompatible with gestalt. If a client goes to see a therapist, the therapist has become an inseparable part of his situation and vice versa. The focus of Husserl's transcendental phenomenology was seeing and understanding the person from an impossibly neutral position from which he could witness *the essence* of the person. He argued that we could suspend our background and our perception of our phenomenal world (van de Riet, 2001). Most gestalt therapists believe that we can limit the influence of the ground of our experience so that we can receive our clients without this material colouring our meeting excessively, but I do not believe that it is possible to suspend our sedimented perceptions of the world completely. Recent neurological research would support this. However, we need to view Husserl's work in the context of the time it was carried out. Even if we accept that his views on phenomenology are incompatible with gestalt, 'Husserl's phenomenology is . . . the founding basis for Gestalt therapy's radicalization of field theory' (McConville, 2001: 200).

Part of Husserl's legacy to gestalt psychotherapy is that whatever is relevant and appropriate to this particular piece of work, its origin is here and now. It exists in the experiential field that is forming around me in the moment as we engage (ibid). Aspects of transcendental phenomenology may not fit neatly with a gestalt philosophy but Husserl's work on bracketing, description and horizontalization provided gestalt with the gift of learning to appreciate the client's reality as far as is possible. To discover more I invite you to turn the page.

54

The discipline of phenomenological reduction

To be open to our client's experience of their world we need to begin by suspending, as far as possible, our own preconceptions of the world. We all interpret our world and to reduce the impact of our interpretations Husserl devised a three-step method. He believed that if we completed the three steps described below, which make up the process of *phenomenological reduction*, also known as *the phenomenological method*, we could then be touched by *the virgin experience*.

Bracketing

All assumptions and expectations concerning how things are or how they should be are set aside through a process of *bracketing*. By this process we put our experience of the world in a pair of brackets so that we can be touched by the client's experience afresh. If this is achieved the therapist's reactions to the experience of meeting the person will not be coloured by their past experience of the world. The therapist will then be as free as possible to meet with the client's experience, and their reactions and impressions will be in response to the client's experience rather than the therapist's perception of the world. We can never be entirely free from our own preconfiguring material, but the process of *bracketing* will alert us to material that may colour the way in which we perceive the client's material and therefore ensure that this material does not contaminate our receiving their experience. Successful bracketing leads to a therapeutic stance of openness to the way in which our client perceives their world.

Description

Having bracketed expectations, don't seek explanations – seek description. The therapist's responses should also be descriptive and focused on what we perceive. If someone is crossing their arms tightly that is what is noticed and described rather than explaining the behaviour as 'defensive' or 'closed'. An example of a phenomenological gestalt 'here and now' experiment that adheres to the rule of description is described in Point 5. Such present-centred, descriptive relating is alien to most in our Western culture and can prove challenging. Also note that people 'describe' their experience through their bodies and the way in which they move, through the inflections in their voice not only through words.

Horizontalization or equalization

Having bracketed assumptions and stayed with immediate description, we then take the stance that anything we see or hear is initially of equal significance. This means that an account of a traumatic event will initially be considered no more or less significant than an uncomfortable shuffling or a distant gaze. The therapist also needs to bear in mind the possible equal importance of what is absent from the dialogue, for instance, if someone seeks therapy following a bereavement but does not discuss aspects of their relationship with the deceased.

The therapist remains open to the client's unfolding story without presuming the next part of the picture even if they imagine that they know the next part of the picture.

Experiential exercise
Stand with your face close to a wall and gradually move backwards. As you move backwards note whether you are expecting or anticipating something coming into your field of vision or whether you are trying to interpret something on the periphery of your field of vision. Attempt to just let things enter your experience from a place of not knowing before letting your attention be drawn in a particular direction.

Most gestalt therapists would agree that we can never be entirely free from assumptions and would align themselves with the idea of being as naïve as possible so that we can then receive as full a sense of the client's phenomenal experience rather than believing that we can transcend all assumptions we have about the world. As Merleau-Ponty so eloquently put it, to 'slacken the threads which attach us to the world' (1962: xiii).

55

Existential phenomenology: 'I am'

The second major branch of phenomenology is existential phenomenology, more commonly known as existentialism. Developed from Husserl's work by his assistant, Martin Heidegger (1889–1976), existential phenomenology holds greater clinical relevance in gestalt therapy. Whereas Husserl focused on *the essence* of being human Heidegger focused on existence, believing that existence precedes essence. From an existential viewpoint Descartes' assertion, 'I think therefore I am' just had the words in the wrong order – I am therefore I think. A concise description of existential phenomenology is given by Merleau-Ponty who describes it as, 'a study of the *advent* of being to consciousness, instead of presuming its possibility as given in advance.' (1962: 61).

Heidegger saw human existence as being tied inseparably to the world. Consequently he did not believe that our existence could be bracketed. Anyone reading Heidegger will come across the German term *Dasein*, and he asserted that 'a human being is a *Dasein*' (Spinelli, 1989: 108), meaning 'being-in-the-world' – this is hyphenated to show the connectedness of our being and the world. The fit with gestalt is again evident in Heidegger's views on seeing our awareness and existence as intersubjective. He saw us as being *thrown* into an uncertain existence that led to death and considered that in order to manage the overwhelming angst and dread aroused by this existential given, we chose to defend against this truth through living *inauthentically*. The effect of living this way is a deadening of our vitality and individuality through rule-bound limitations. Conversely, if we live authentically we acknowledge our sense of agency and responsibility in our lives.

Gestalt therapy seeks to heighten awareness so that the client can choose whether to live authentically or inauthentically. With existentialism key to the stance of the gestalt therapist, we seek to increase freedom of choice. By this I do not mean that we can always choose the events that happen to us, but we do choose our reaction to the event and the meaning we give to it. A colloquial example of such choice is whether we see the glass as half full or half empty in a given situation.

Owning our freedom of choice means living authentically and this does bring its problems in that we cannot presuppose any outcome or belief, including that life has meaning. The meaning we make is constructed by us. Whether we search for meaning in the Bible, the Koran, philosophy or the Sunday supplement, existentialism holds that ultimately our existence is meaningless. In order to live authentically, to be, we must accept the uncertainty of existence.

Existential phenomenology is the phenomenology of being-in-the-world and as such defines existence as relational. It is precisely the client's process of relating with the world that is of interest to gestalt therapists. Existential phenomenology is an instrument of inquiry into my dialogue with the world and my world's dialogue with me. From an existential perspective we are ultimately alone with the meanings that we give to our experience and to things. No one can experience what we experience in our separate life-spaces. Although I need others to exist, in this sense I exist in isolation. Awareness of meaninglessness, Heidegger argues, leads to nothingness as we recognize our temporary existence with the only certainty being death. Along with such uncertainty comes *angst*, if we accept our freedom of choice, responsibility, the meaninglessness of our existence and our ultimate isolation. To live authentically means facing these existential issues, the alternative is to live inauthentically.

I am painting a bleak picture of our existence. Quite frankly, from this brief account of existential phenomenology and our being-in-the-world, I think that I might sooner live my life inauthentically! However, paradoxically in our separateness there is togetherness. We are all in the same boat and although we may all have a different experience of that boat, through dialogue we can experience something of the other's perception and their being-in-the-world. Our respective realities and perceptions are co-created within our intersubjective dance with the world and no one's view of reality is any more real than anyone else's. It follows therefore that in gestalt therapy the therapist's reality is no more or less valid than the client's.

56

Intersubjectivity: I am always embedded in my experience

As we have seen in the last point, you have your subjective experience of the world and I have my subjective experience of the world. The world may be made up of a multitude of subjective selves each making sense of their own experience and this may suggest that individuals walk the earth as separate atomized individuals disconnected from one another. However, anyone who has ever felt tearful in response to another's grief, angry at another's injustice or whose heart has raced with another's excitement will have an embodied sense that this is not so. We discover who we are in relationship by dialoguing with our respective fields of experience.

When we talk about phenomenology in gestalt therapy there is a danger that we place our focus solely on the client, observing and working with their awareness continuum without due consideration to what is happening *between* client and therapist. Whilst we work in the service of the client, our subjective reactions in the meeting provide us with information. Of course, we do need to ensure that we are not responding to our own proactive material and this is why we need regular supervision coupled with our own personal therapy. In gestalt therapy 'clinical phenomenology is a two-person practice' (Yontef, 2002: 19), through dialogue we explore the phenomenology of the relationship. I have my experience of the meeting and you have yours, I explore with you what meaning we create and how it is created.

It is the intersubjective relational patterns that emerge between client and therapist, with attention to the minutiae of these patterns in the here and now, together with how these patterns repeat in the client's wider field of relationships that are of interest to the gestalt therapist. By its very nature gestalt's views on self as process constitute human beings as intersubjective beings. That we live and breathe in an intersubjective field of relations becomes more obvious to us the more often we meet with difference. If I meet with someone from a radically different culture, my different world-view is brought more sharply into focus, as is the way we then make sense of our respective worlds in the meeting.

> The human organism/environment is, of course, not only physical but social. So in any humane study . . . we must speak of a field in which at least social-cultural, animal and physical factors interact.
>
> (PHG, 1951: 228)

PHG go on to say that when we encounter novelty, such as when I meet you and you meet me, the novelty needs to be assimilated. This process of assimilation leads to '*creative adjustment of the organism and the environment*' (PHG, 1951: 230, original italics). When we meet we are both changed in that meeting; the change might be a hardening or softening of the contact boundary. From a gestalt perspective on-going change between subjectivities is inevitable because of our view that reality, meaning and experience are *co-created* in the *between* of the relationship.

As I write I am aware of a feeling of gratitude and humility surfacing in relation to many of the clients I have worked with over the years. Some stand out more than others but all these intersubjective meetings changed me in some way just as my meeting those clients changed them. I also change as I remember the experience of those meetings and I imagine that the people I am remembering do too as they look back. These experiences emerge from the interactions I have enjoyed within the intersubjective field of my work as a therapist. 'Experiencing emerges out of *interactions* within the intersubjective field, and behavior and experience can be understood only in the context of that field' (Jacobs 1992: 27, original italics). Hence, my experience and that of my client's can only be understood within the context of each of these relationships or within the context of my remembering these relationships now.

The notion of self as relational and interdependent with others is supported in physics. Quantum theory shows we can never end up with separate things; you always deal with interconnections. As well as the gestalt saying that one thing leads to another, it is also true that one thing affects another.

57

Attending to the bodily 'felt sense'

Gestalt therapy is a body-oriented therapy; with its philosophy of holism and phenomenology it cannot be anything else, for when we refer to the term 'body' or 'bodywork' we refer to a unitary being as part of a unified field. In gestalt and phenomenology we use the terms *the living* or *lived body*. This may sound strange at first but the reason these terms are used is to emphasize that we work with a body of experience, a body that carries with it a history and is inseparable from the matrix of relationships it is embedded in. The gestalt therapist tries to make contact with the *actual living* of the client in the here and now, to increase awareness of, and experiment with, the person's rhythms and patterns of living (PHG, 1951). These patterns of contact and withdrawal manifest in the client's bodily movements, both subtle and obvious, and in their manifestation reflect the client's bodily felt sense – a felt sense that may not necessarily be in conscious awareness. As gestalt therapists we do not need to seek to uncover what is underneath a bodily felt sense, a movement or a gesture but work with it. A gesture that appears to hit out or reach out speaks to me but I do not look for anything underneath it but work with the presenting phenomena, allowing space for any awareness of meaning to emerge in the client. In the moment, 'Things are entirely what they appear to be and behind them ... there is nothing' (Sartre, 1948).

It is often useful for the client to move in order to increase their awareness of their environment and their body in relation to their environment. Indeed, physical movement often brings about psychological movement, illustrating the unitary nature of our being. A person's perception of their body and of objects in contact with the body is vague when there is no movement (Goldstein, 1939).

We gain a bodily felt sense through lived experience rather than 'talking about' an experience. When I 'talk about' an experience I am one step removed from that experience – I am thinking about it, rather than living it – as such the way in which this 'talked about' experience touches or affects me is diluted. It is the difference between talking about being held by your partner and allowing yourself to truly be held by your partner. Hence, in gestalt therapy we seek to increase the client's bodily felt sense by encouraging immediate relating, heightening awareness of contact functions and modelling an embodied way of being, for when we habitually place our experience at a disembodied distance we diminish ourselves. Of course, this is not a unilaterally negative movement; as ever, behaviour is field contextual. If I am encountering a traumatic situation, an ability to move away from my bodily felt sense will probably be what my situation calls for and this is a valuable ability. However, this is also what our Western culture usually calls for. Consequently, I believe that for most of us our growing edge in relation to a disembodiment–embodiment awareness continuum is in a movement towards the embodiment end of that continuum through heightening our awareness of our bodily felt sense.

Experiential exercise
Walk around the room slowly paying attention to the way in which you distribute your weight. What areas of your body hold tension and what areas are you less aware of? Slowly move through muscle groups from your feet and calves up to your forehead. You could even make statements from these different areas of you body in relation to your felt sense – in the first person of course! Just notice what information your lived body holds.

58

Projective identification

There is a variety of definitions given in gestalt and beyond for the concept of projective identification. Let me offer a brief but by no means comprehensive cross-section of the diverse views of this process.

The term projective identification was first used by Melanie Klein (1946), a pioneer from the object relations school of psychoanalysis, where it has frequently been described as a 'primitive defence mechanism' – meaning that the process originated early in child development.

Some of the descriptions of the process offered by a selection of gestalt writers are as follows:

* Philippson says that, 'the therapist will find herself experiencing emotions which are being suppressed by the client' (2001: 80) and further describes projective identification as, 'the therapist picking up feelings that originate in the client' (ibid: 116).
* Joyce and Sills (2001) discuss the concept as 'carrying' a disowned feeling for the client and direct the reader towards the object relationalist Ogden (1982) who in turn describes the process as, 'a concept that addresses the way in which feeling states corresponding to the unconscious fantasies of one person (the projector) are engendered in and processed by another person (the recipient), that is, the way in which one person makes use of another person to experience and contain an aspect of himself.'
* MacKewn (1997: 95) describes the process, 'whereby a client unawarely conveys his/her feelings by "giving" the therapist an experience of how he/she feels, rather than by articulating'. She goes on to clarify that the therapist does not actually feel the client's feelings but that similar feelings are evoked.
* Staemmler (1993) shared his thoughts in his comprehensive paper by discussing projective identification in terms of an

'interaction pattern' and saw the 'communicative function' of the process as the basis of its therapeutic potential.

- Yontef (1993) describes the process of projective identification as the person alienating or disowning an aspect of themselves, attributing it to the other person and then instead of moving away from that person identifying with them. A bright person who does not own her intelligence may project that quality onto the other.

In my years as a gestalt trainer and supervisor, I have no doubt that of all the concepts and processes people have struggled to comprehend in grappling with psychotherapy and gestalt theory it is the concept of projective identification that has caused the most confusion. Perusing the small sample of definitions above perhaps we can see why. Whilst I am sure that Ogden's thinking is fine for the modality for which it was intended, to my mind this particular piece of psychoanalytic thinking does not transport into gestalt. It fails to acknowledge the co-created nature of experience, is not phenomenological or field theoretical. Other definitions do to a greater or lesser extent acknowledge these areas. However, I believe that the processes discussed could be just as adequately described in terms of counter-transference or co-transference. The use of these terms better illuminates a relational dynamic whereas describing projective identification can lead to the belief that the client simply puts a feeling into the therapist (it is invariably spoken of this way round). There is no doubt that gestalt theory has been enriched by the importation of psychoanalytic concepts, but we do need to carefully consider how these concepts rest with the fundamental principles of gestalt.

Perhaps the recent discoveries of mirror neurons (Schore, 2003) which show something of how we understand one another's mental states, throw a different light on such processes as projective identification in that the co-created nature of such a phenomenon is becoming increasingly evident.

I recall a workshop I attended run by a renowned gestalt therapist and trainer at a recent conference. A participant, himself a well-known and respected trainer, questioned the workshop leader about a particular process and described it as projective identification. The leader's response was swift, 'I suggest you find another way of conceptualizing that,' she replied. Knowing the participant I don't think that he had any intention of conceptualizing his views on projective identification any differently. In microcosm in that interaction I witnessed the diversity of views within gestalt that enriches the approach, leads to lively debate but which also confuses its students.

59

Energy, interests, needs, vitality

My wife and I took our four-year-old granddaughter to the zoo; she rushed around excitedly and was particularly wide-eyed and captivated by the meerkats, having never seen one before. Whilst delighted by our granddaughter's enthusiasm, my wife and I walked around at a more leisurely pace and although we found them interesting, we had both seen meerkats before.

We see energy, interest and vitality on the surface of the other. The brightness of a person's eyes, the quality of their voice, the nature of their movements, the way they hold their body all reflect the quality of contact with their environment. Our energy, interest and vitality are stimulated and increased when we encounter the novel. When energized we can move more freely to contact our environment to meet our needs. If sufficiently supported in our life situation we are able to invest in constructively aggressing upon our environment (see Point 76). Contact with the novel will generate excitement and energy. We become motivated to satisfy our needs and to follow our interests. Change becomes possible through the aggressive action of deconstructing fixed gestalts, completing unfinished business – to follow a contact sequence through (see Points 13 and 14). If supportive field conditions are absent, or perceived as being absent, fluidity is lost. The energy that creates excitement in the well-supported person creates anxiety or depression in the under-supported person. In the well-supported person it leads to expansion of their perceived lifespace, in the under-supported person contraction.

When a person feels unsupported in journeying beyond their familiarity boundary, through fear and anxiety they restrict them-selves in relation to their environment. In the absence of sufficient support, even minor challenges can seem daunting and may be avoided. Self-belief can be lost as the choice is made to live life in shades of grey leading to stagnation and a deadening of any vibrancy. Energy might appear to be absent but can be directed inwards or invested in moderations to contact that work to substitute the known for the unknown even though the known is incongruent with the present situation.

When working with clients the gestalt therapist needs to pay attention to the client's energy flow. We might begin by noticing where energy appears to be present or blocked in the client's body; noticing what level of energy and vitality is co-created in the session between therapist and client. Noting when energy drops and when it increases and noting energy patterns in response to fulfilling needs (and what sort of needs) can give indications of areas for attention. Structured awareness experiments exploring bodily energy fields can also be useful in making a process diagnosis upon which to base interventions.

As therapists we need to pay attention to our own flow of energy. Treat a loss of interest as information in considering its meaning and view any variations in interest or vitality as a function of the field to explore either with the client or in supervision. One way in which we can stifle the life out of therapy is by becoming dogmatic about our theories. Let us learn our theories well but have the wisdom to let go of them when they block inventiveness and vitality.

60

Awareness and diminished awareness

> The moment one gives close attention to anything, even a blade of grass, it becomes a mysterious, awesome, indescribably magnificent world in itself.
>
> (H. Miller, 1957)

Just as we are always in contact so we are always aware, and just as the quality of our contact will slide along a continuum, so will the degree and quality of our awareness. We have seen some of the ways in which we diminish our awareness through moderating contact with our environment (see Part 1) and how contact with the novel can stimulate us.

To illustrate a healthy flow of awareness and diminished awareness let me return to the story of my granddaughter at the zoo discussed in the last point. When she was absorbed in her experience watching the meerkats they were the figural element in her awareness; my wife and I were a dimmer awareness in her background. When she eventually tired of watching the meerkats she turned towards us to move on and we became the sharp figure of her awareness with the meerkats now in her ground. Later she returned home and shared the experience with her mother, whilst doing so she was aware of the memory of what she saw and also aware of her contact with her mother. Hence, she had full awareness of both her memory of the past event and of being in full contact with her mother in the present. In figure and ground terms she would have rapidly and seamlessly shuttled between these two types of awareness as she shared her experience of the meerkats.

When our awareness is increased new gestalts form and in this process an integration of what was previously experienced as separate elements of the field takes place. An increased awareness can result in a complete reorganization of the person's perceptual field, their old tried and trusted ways of viewing their situation are thrown into question. The process can be similar to that of a scientific discovery that blows asunder previously held beliefs, and the resistance to such an emerging awareness can be just as fierce. Excitement can turn into its close bedfellow anxiety if the client is insufficiently supported during such shifts. Increasing the client's awareness can bring about spontaneous change and if the field is unsupportive of this change clients may choose to diminish their awareness.

Such a movement needs to be considered in the context of the client's situation with respect for their ability to self-regulate. I recall a useful diminishing of my emotional awareness in the days that followed my father's death. I was able to engage in the 'business end of things', helping to arrange the funeral, arranging time away from work and cover for clients. However, it would have been a problem had I maintained my level of diminished awareness beyond this acute period of grief.

I would like to invite you to engage in two exercises, the first focusing on the value of diminishing awareness through moderations to contact, the second designed to increase awareness.

Experiential exercise 1
Complete the following sentences with examples from your experience (you may wish to refer back to Points 15 to 19):
A field-congruent way of me diminishing my awareness through desensitization is . . .
Then repeat through all other moderations to contact – deflection, introjection, retroflection, projection, confluence and egotism.

Experiential exercise 2
Take a piece of fruit and find a quiet place. I'd like you to spend ten minutes exploring this piece of fruit without eating it. Use your senses to fully explore it. Notice when your awareness drifts away or is interrupted (for example, with thoughts of 'oh, this is silly!' or what you will do next), pay attention to any fluctuations in your awareness.

The second exercise conflicts with our cultural norms and so may seem quite 'foreign'. In therapy sessions we could work to heighten a client's awareness through using an adapted version of this exercise in relation to awareness 'blind spots', for example in relation to how the client holds his/her body.

61

Patterns of contacting

As we have seen, it is the therapist's responsibility to bracket as far as possible any material that will preconfigure the ground of their meeting with the client. What the therapist will be touched by if they can achieve this stance will be the way the client has settled in their way of being in relation to their world, what Merleau-Ponty (1962) referred to as their *sedimented* beliefs or outlook. We all carry such beliefs and they form the basis of how we make sense of our situation.

Regarding sedimentation let me draw an analogy with wine making. In the making of wine the sediment needs to be given sufficient time to settle, once it has settled the wine will clear. Let us consider this process in terms of figure and ground. The gradually clearing figure (the wine) forms and becomes increasingly clear from the ground (the sediment, the demijohn and everything outside the demijohn). As long as the sediment is undisturbed the wine will continue to clear. However, if the wine is disturbed the sediment will have to settle again and each particle of the sediment will settle differently to how it was before. To continue with my analogy, the ground will have changed and a different clarity (figure) will need to form against a different ground. The new figure and ground will need to sediment down over time.

In essence gestalt therapy is a phenomenological investigation into how the client is selfing in relation to their situation. The way in which the client organizes his world, what patterns he creates and what creative adjustments are at play. As such we could refer to gestalt therapy as 'gestalting therapy' (L. Perls, 1992: 21).

The patterns the client and therapist create in relating in therapy can be seen as clues as to how the client configures their relationships outside the therapy room. We could view patterns of contacting across a range of gestalt theoretical maps such as those discussed in Part 1. What is crucial in our relational therapy is that we recognize that there are two contacting styles in the room. How I reach out to make contact with the client will affect how they reach out to make contact with me and everything outside the room will impact this contacting process. My way of being will invite certain patterns of responses. If we talk of the client 'being in' a parent transference or erotic transference, we tell only part of the story.

There are patterns of relating and perception that we all have in common. In gestalt psychology the fundamental principle of gestalt perception is the law of Pragnanz, which states that we tend to order our experience in a manner that is regular, orderly, symmetric and simple.

Figure 3.2

Figure 3.3

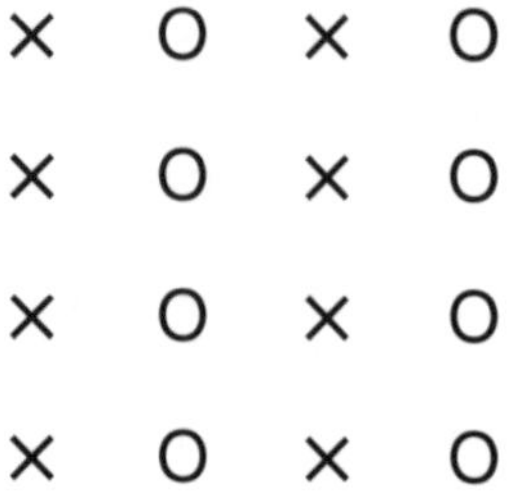

×	O	×	O
×	O	×	O
×	O	×	O
×	O	×	O

Figure 3.4

```
X  0  X  0

X  0  X  0

X  0  X  0

X  0  X  0
```

Figure 3.5

- The Law of Closure – We make sense of images by closing any gaps that may be missing in order to complete a regular figure. In Figures 3.2 and 3.3 the gaps are filled to complete the images of a circle and a horse with rider.
- The Law of Continuity – We perceive things as continuing even though this may not literally be what is evident – another element in perceiving Figures 3.2 and 3.3.
- The Law of Similarity – Similar elements or patterns are grouped together. The similarity might be form, colour or shape in a diagrammatic example. In Figure 3.4 we tend to group the images together in columns rather than in rows.
- The Law of Proximity – Elements will be grouped in relation to proximity; consequently in Figure 3.5 we tend to see four rows rather than four columns.
- The Law of Symmetry – We perceive symmetrical images as belonging together regardless of their distance.

These 'laws' will be at play in how we pattern, order and form the gestalting of our experience.

62

Working with dreams

Fritz Perls described dreams as 'the royal road to integration' (Perls, 1969: 66). He viewed them as existential messages, something of a commentary on the person's way of being in the world. He saw dreams primarily as projections in that everything contained in the dream was a representation of an aspect of the dreamer. Consequently, his style of working with dreams followed the methodology of working with projection. This method involves the client talking in the first person from different aspects of the dream, possibly dialoguing with other aspects of the dream. A delightful example of Perls working with a dream as projection is shared by Polster and Polster. A client dreams he is leaving a therapy session and goes for a walk in the park.

> . . he goes across the bridle path, into the park. So I ask him, 'Now play the bridle path.' He answered indignantly, 'What? And let everybody shit and crap on me?' You see, he really got the identification.
>
> (Polster and Polster, 1973: 266)

In gestalt therapy the meaning of the dream needs to surface from the client. Our task is to facilitate this process with the client to heighten their awareness of the unique meaning of the dream images for them at this point in time, not to interpret the dream. We need to bracket any assumptions that surface.

Working with dreams as projection is only one way of working with a dream. Isadore From worked with dreams viewing them through a lens of retroflection, seeing the retroflection as being a turning away from an expression to a significant other. However, we could view a dream through a lens of any combination of the moderations to contact. The dream can also be seen as a field event and may be compared to the person's waking life if there is a stark contrast between the two.

The common ground for whatever way we work with a dream

is that it is viewed as an integration of disparate parts of the self. From a viewpoint of self as process these disparate parts will exist in the person's relationship with their situation rather than in the person in isolation.

The starting point for whatever way we work with a dream is usually to increase the immediacy of relating the dream by inviting the client to tell the dream in the first person using here and now language. Some broad guidelines for working with a client on a dream are:

- Check out the immediate post-dream feeling.
- Give the client the choice of where to start.
- Stay with the process of the dream and the telling of the dream rather than the content. Note the mood and 'flavour' of the dream and the reactions it evokes in you.
- Begin where there is most energy, but note where there are fluctuations in energy. High energy does not always equate to the most important/relevant.
- Powerful material can be evoked, so it is important that adequate time is left at the end of the session to ground the client and debrief.

Some options for facilitating the exploration of dreams in therapy are:

1. Setting up a dream dialogue where the whole dream is spoken to, for example, as an empty chair experiment.
2. Working with elements of the dream as projected parts of the dreamer, as discussed above.
3. Re-enacting the dream. This would usually be done in a group with attention paid to the qualities group members have that attract the various elements of the dream. A re-enactment of a dream can be done in 1:1 therapy using creative media such as shells or sand tray to represent the elements.
4. Unfinished dreams can be continued in therapy beyond the point of 'and then I woke up'. The client would be invited to continue in the first person.
5. Attention can focus on the client's bodily sensation and reactions as they tell or remember the dream. Alternatively

the dream can be expressed bodily through movement or taking up different postures.

6. Creative media can be used as a non-verbal expression of the dream – clay, paints, sand tray, etc.
7. If a client doesn't remember their dreams they can be invited into an experiment where they dialogue with the absent dream.

Some ways of working with dreams are more individualistic than others. It is useful to hold the question of what is the meaning of this dream in relation to the client's wider situation.

Dialogue: emerging through relationship

63

Martin Buber: I–Thou and I–It relating

In the beginning is relation.

(Buber, 1958:18)

Martin Buber (1878–1965) was an existentialist, philosopher and a prolific writer. His work on the philosophical articulation of the dialogic principle has been integrated into, and expanded, in gestalt therapy and in particular his poetic thesis on human existence *I and Thou* (1958). One of the founders of gestalt therapy, Laura Perls, reported that a personal meeting with Buber profoundly influenced her. Gestalt is indebted to Buber's work for its values of presence, confirmation, authenticity, dialogue and inclusion.

I–Thou and I–It represent the two polar relational stances as the two primary attitudes that humans hold towards one another. It is between these poles that the natural flow of connection and separation takes place; both are essential in the give and take of human relating. This flow is essentially what we refer to in gestalt when we talk of dialogue. Buber says that all living is meeting, and these relational stances represent the attitude of that meeting. The hyphen between these two terms holds specific significance for it represents our eternal connectedness to the other and our world. According to Buber there is no 'I' that stands alone.

The necessity and inevitability of I–It relating has not always been fully recognized in the gestalt literature. I–It relating is an essential pole in the process of dialogue, being required for 'such functions as judgement, will, orientation and reflection' (Farber, 1966, quoted in Hycner and Jacobs, 1985: 52) and involves self-consciousness and the awareness of separation (Friedman, 1976, ibid). In I–It relating we are objectifying, goal oriented, concerned with doing rather than being. The task becomes figural whilst the other recedes into the ground. Such objectifying is a necessary part of relating. 'The ontological character of existence requires both distance and relation.' (Buber, 1965a: 61–62).

Whilst I–It relating may be a necessary part of our existence, it is only a part. We need separation *and* connection. However, we are living in times where an illusion of contact can masquerade in a multitude of forms of virtual contact. Isolation, detachment and alienation can become 'comfortable' options whilst intimacy and closeness can become increasingly unfamiliar alternatives. As we create more and more sophisticated ways of keeping our distance we '. . . split not only *between* persons, not only in our relationship *with* nature, but also *within* our own psyches.' (Hycner, 1993: 5, original italics).

> Without It a human being cannot live. But whoever lives with only that is not human.
>
> (Buber, 1958: 85)

There has probably never been a greater need to redress the relational imbalance through building the ground to facilitate I–Thou dialogue than there is today. So let me clarify what the I–Thou relationship is.

Whilst the I–It stance is concerned with doing and achieving in the relationship, the I–Thou is a state of *being* in relationship. The I–Thou relation trusts the between and is therefore willing to surrender to that between and in that surrender the other's humanness is affirmed. An I–Thou meeting can only take place when both parties are willing to surrender to the between, it cannot be forced or coaxed. As Buber states, it comes through grace. Many clients that walk through our doors have been starved of such relating, they are not in a position to surrender to the between of a relationship to gain the nourishment they yearn. It is through the therapist's willingness to hold an I–Thou attitude during I–It relating, to reach out and be available to the client without the expectation of being met that creates the ground for profound relational healing.

One of the ironies in this paradoxical profession is that if we aim for I–Thou relating or I–Thou moments, we immediately objectify the I–Thou, resulting in I–It relating. It is also the destiny of every I–Thou encounter to recede into our past, become a memory, perhaps to be treasured, perhaps vaguely remembered or to have its passing grieved over, but related to as a thing nevertheless, an event – an It.

64

The between

> *Somewhere in the in-between,*
> *Atoms bouncing, yet unseen,*
> *Not created by you or me,*
> *But fused together from the 'we',*
> *In grace they meet, with grace they move,*
> *Our energies, Our hearts, Our truths,*
> *Tentatively these atoms slide, for there is a pull to hide,*
> *Yet magically – I know not how,*
> *Your 'I' glides to meet my 'Thou'.*

Clients first coming to therapy often seek explanation for their experience. The gestalt therapist does not explain – any attempts to do so would merely be the therapist's interpretation. Neither is explanation uncovered or discovered as this assumes that there is a pre-existing reason for the client's experience. Explanation, if needed, emerges and is created *between* client and therapist.

In a dialogic relationship with another we readily recognize that there are two realities but there is also a third reality that emerges in the between of that relationship. That reality is greater than the sum of its parts. It emerges in the meeting and has the power to change both the therapist and the client, providing both have sufficiently permeable contact boundaries. In gestalt we are interested in what happens intersubjectively, we therefore pay close attention to what emerges, and how this emerges, between therapist and client rather than focusing solely on the client. This is because we believe that in engaging in dialogue meaning is not found in one person or the other, 'nor in both together, but only in the dialogue itself, in the "between" which they live together' (Buber, 1965a: 25). When we meet there we both change as the material that creates our personal worlds reconfigures in relation to the other.

What happens between client and therapist will depend, amongst other factors, upon the therapeutic philosophy of the gestalt therapist. Some prefer a more active, experimental and directly challenging approach with a greater focus on ego functioning (see Point 7). Whilst those from the relational gestalt schools focus more on id functioning, fore-contact, gradual mobilization and receptivity towards the client's subjective experience. 'There is an emphasis on support rather than challenge with a greater tolerance of confluence amongst relational schools' (Denham-Vaughan, 2005: 11).

If we take an intersubjective view of the world of relationships, experience and behaviour can only be understood in the context of the client's situation. It follows that any diagnostic picture can only be formed in relation to the client's situation. This reality is formed in the between of his situation.

There is a moment in reaching out to contact the other when we let go of our independent existence with no guarantee that we will be met. This moment of letting go can hold some of the terrors of the impasse for both therapist and client. We may be tempted to adopt a 'professional' way of being, fall back on techniques or distance ourselves through questioning the client. Whilst questioning and technique has its place in the work of the therapist, if the call from the client is for relationship we need to be willing to let go of them, 'The deciding reality is the therapist not the methods . . . I am for methods, but just in order to use them not believe in them' (Buber 1967: 164).

65

Inclusion – a cautionary note regarding empathy

Inclusion is when the therapist honours the phenomenological experience of the client without letting go of his own phenomenological experience. We need to respectfully enter the world of the client to experience, as far as possible, their perception within their lifespace without judging, analysing or interpreting whilst retaining a sense of our own separate, autonomous existence. The gestalt therapist does not impose their beliefs on the client's experience of their situation; the starting point is always to listen to the client's story whilst noting how they and the client are impacted. In inclusion we are seeking the meaning for the client whilst noting the information present in our reactions. To do so we need to shuttle between the experienced world of the client and the experienced world of the therapist. In empathy the latter is subsumed whereas in inclusion we experience the other *and* distance from the other. However, empathy can be seen as a starting point for the practice of inclusion as Jacobs considers that 'without empathic underpinnings, no true dialogue can take place' (1995: 153).

The literal meaning of empathy is to feel into the other, and can be colloquially described as putting yourself in another's shoes. Although the term is often used more loosely, it means journeying over to the other and leaving your side. Inclusion on the other hand is 'a bold swinging – demanding the most intensive stirring of one's own being – into the life of the other' (Buber, 1965a: 81).

Perls wrote 'If a therapist withholds himself in empathy, he deprives the field of its main instrument'. He goes on to say that a gestalt therapist 'must have a relational awareness of the whole situation' (1973: 105); central to the 'whole situation' is the therapist's perceptions and reactions. Buber saw empathy as an important *feeling* but that by its very nature this feeling ignored one existential pole of the dialogue. He saw inclusion as an existential movement towards attempting to experience both sides of the dialogue. Inclusion involves the embodiment of the other's experience whilst not losing a sense of one's own embodied experience. I use the term 'embodied' here to emphasize that inclusion is more than a cognitive or psychological process – when we are inclusive of the other we soften our contact boundary and allow the other to stir our whole being.

'The therapist must feel the other side, the patient's side of the relationship, as a bodily touch to know how the patient feels it' (Buber, 1967: 173). This statement could describe empathy with the emphasis placed on the client and we can find many similar statements in gestalt as empathy describes *part of* the process of inclusion. I do not agree with Buber's belief that we can '*know* how the patient feels' as I do not believe that we can ever fully know another's experience – we can only gain an *as if* quality of their experience and existence. Even if I'm mistaken I believe that to hold an element of doubt about my capacity to know another is a healthy relational stance that safeguards the client and the therapeutic relationship from non-inclusive narcissistically oriented relating.

If the therapy relationship were mutually fully inclusive, Buber would say that it was not therapy. This would tally with the over-simplistic notion that when a client begins to consistently genuinely inquire about the therapist then therapy is over. Although some clients are probably well capable of practising inclusion with the therapist, they would not be serving their best interests to do so (Jacobs, 1995). Hence, Buber describes the therapeutic relationship as a one-sided inclusion in which the therapist strives to practise the art and the client receives.

66

Presence

I sat with a colleague today and with this particular point in mind asked, 'Pat, if you were a psychotherapy student what would you want to know about presence?' After a thoughtful pause she replied, 'I'd want to know what it was.' Fair point, I thought, but as our conversation unfolded, a clear and concise theoretical definition of this aspect of dialogue was not easily forthcoming. Then, with some synchronicity, I happened upon a paper by Chidiac and Denham-Vaughan (2007) who shared something of our struggle in stating that although they could name presence and describe it, giving a clear theoretical exposition of what can seem an 'ethereal notion' was a different matter. A further thought then occurred to me as a result of these two 'meetings': that I am dependent upon others' presence in order to make sense of my world. Their presence – actual, imagined or remembered – helps me make sense of my experience.

Of course, we will always be present in one sense but as with all aspects of our being we can show our presence authentically or inauthentically (Heidegger, 1962). If I am with another and feel one reaction but present another, I am relating inauthentically. The therapist shows caring through honesty rather than constant softness. A real meeting of persons may mean giving feedback that the other does not want to hear, and sometimes this feedback may be misheard as rejection. The therapist expresses them-selves judiciously and with graded discrimination. The therapist expresses feelings, observations, preferences, personal experience and thoughts and thereby models phenomenological reporting. However, we will meet with a variety of different clients with differing relational needs during the course of our work and this will call for us to calibrate our presence upwards or downwards. It is part of the gestalt therapist's task to assess in each passing moment to what degree to show their presence and when to subsume it and to continually reassess this. If we calibrate our presence too far upwards, some of the possible consequences are that the client is overwhelmed, does not feel that there is sufficient space for them or feels themselves diminished. Tiptoe around, showing your presence too carefully and the client may feel unseen, unheard or that the therapist lacks interest. Each miscalibration can trigger a shame response in the client.

Being present is more than simply being with; it is being with and available with all that you are in a fully embodied way: cognitively, emotionally, spiritually. When I am practising presence I am not being present for myself and neither am I being present solely for the client, I am practising presence for that third reality – the 'between' in the service of the client. As I write it feels wrong to say that I *practise* presence, for in the give and take of the therapeutic relationship when I give myself over to the relationship it can feel effortless. This sense of effortlessness is probably due to the unfolding nature of presence. If I aim for presence I move into pretence and make a movement away from the client and being authentic. I am moving towards some picture of being in this relationship rather than simply being in this relationship.

There are clinical decisions to be made regarding use of presence and we need to be guided by the client before us. A higher calibration of presence may involve self-disclosure of various forms, whilst calibrating our presence downwards may mean retroflecting or minimizing an emotional reponse to a client, perhaps because of the developmental stage of the relationship. Presence involves being and doing and as such has been summed up as 'energetic availability and fluid responsiveness' (Chidiac and Denham-Vaughan, 2007) and likened to the middle mode of functioning where 'the spontaneous is both active and passive, both willing and done to' (PHG, 1951: 154).

Buber suggested that the relational therapist needs to develop a *detached presence*. In suggesting this paradoxical position he was referring to the need for the therapist to be able to reflect upon what is happening at that moment in the relationship whilst being fully present in the relationship. I see this process as a very rapid shuttling between presence and a form of egotism where the therapist 'helicopters' above the relationship to reflect on what is happening in that moment.

67

Confirmation

Confirmation is the acknowledgement of one's whole being. The need for confirmation in many people is so great that if they fail to gain confirmation for whom they are, they will seek confirmation for who they imagine the other will want them to be and adapt accordingly. In the therapy room clients with a developmental lack of confirmation may be on the lookout for how to be a 'good client'. The therapist needs to consider how they may inadvertently support this. We need to affirm the separate existence of the other with all that means: uniqueness, separateness, difference, acceptance, and connectedness.

To confirm the other we need to, as far as possible, enter the phenomenological world of the client bracketing our judgements. Confirmation occurs within the I-Thou moment. However, it is not just restricted to this peak moment in therapy but is held within the fibre of the dialogic attitude. If I meet the other with respect and appreciation of their otherness, with an attitude of equality, then I believe that the client can feel confirmed in their humanness. Often the process of confirming the other is written about in absolute terms. I am not one for absolutes. Perhaps we need to consider degrees of confirmation, thinking in terms of a continuum.

Often in life we get confirmed as a person conditionally: as a good athlete, a good son/daughter, a good parent, a good therapist and so on. This conditional confirmation is for how well the role is fulfilled from the perception of the one confirming, not for the person. The process can parallel in therapy with the 'good client' being the client who is 'confirmed' for what they are rather than who they are. So how do we confirm clients who push every boundary? Confirmation is about confirming the client's existence rather than their behaviour. Consequently, the therapist can be confirming the client for who they are whilst not necessarily approving, and maybe challenging, what they are doing.

There are two acts in confirming another. First it takes an act of will to turn towards the other – with the willingness to confirm present in the therapist's ground. Second, the act of confirmation is achieved through grace – it cannot be forced. As a result the healing of past relational ruptures can take place through such meeting. If we are to be congruent with the gestalt theory of self as process, confirmation is an on-going process rather than being something we do and move on from to some other relational task. It is a relational attitude that needs to pervade the whole therapy situation. There needs to be an over-arching confirming attitude to support the client at those inevitable times when the client feels missed, shamed, guilty or just plain wrong.

A lack of confirmation in early developmental years has been closely linked with 'mental illness' or 'psychopathology' and has been defined by Hycner (1993) as being a result of an early aborted dialogue. Trub (1952) paints a tragic picture of a chronic retroflection supported by core introjects through such deprivation when he shared his belief that in the deepest reaching out to others the person has not been heard, resulting in the only option available to the child, that her voice has been turned tragically inwards. Perhaps it is beyond us as therapists to facilitate a full reparation of such passive atrocities, but we can confirm the client for all that they are in the present, including their creativity in surviving such enduring trauma.

68

Commitment to dialogue

The first question that arises for me when committing to anything is what am I committing to? The term 'dialogue' commonly means to use language. Although we invariably relate with language, in gestalt therapy our view of dialogue is wider, there is non-verbal dialogue that takes place in every meeting. Dialogue as discussed by Buber and practised in gestalt therapy is marked by a turning of the therapist's being towards the client's being with honesty and openness in the service of the relationship. We acknowledge our common humanity and horizontalize the relationship through the dialogical. Because dialogue reaches out to the other beyond words, it is difficult to express fully in words: 'Dialogue has an aesthetic quality that I am unable to define or describe adequately; it stirs my soul and involves me totally' (Korb, 1999). It may follow that we know that we are not committed to dialogue when we are not stirred in such a way.

In committing to dialogue we enter a shared situation and one that reaches beyond the dyad. We need to appreciate the impact of the client's wider field upon them. I have already voiced some of the possible pitfalls of the individualistic ground upon which we walk and how this conflicts with a gestalt philosophy. To reiterate briefly we can treat the client as a completely separate entity, which could potentially lead to a separation of their problem from their wider situation. There is a danger that we can parallel this process by isolating the therapeutic dyad (or group) in creating some sort of illusory therapy bubble, separate from the client's situation. We are dialoguing with a client who is dialoguing with a whole situation; we cannot meaningfully dialogue with a client detached from his situation. When we dialogue with a person, we dialogue with a whole field of relations.

A commitment to dialogue is a commitment to the between of the relationship. It is this 'between' that guides the therapist as patterns of relating form and difference is acknowledged. It is not until we encounter difference that we know that we exist and we expand our experiential worlds the more we are in contact with difference. The more resistant we are to any difference the more rigid and fixed our contact boundaries become – witness the fixed and rigid views in prejudice and racism. Consequently, the process of dialogue is more valued in gestalt than any particular outcome and is more valued than either the client or the therapist individually. We use the dialogue to serve the client and remain creatively indifferent to any outcomes.

Many clients are not available for dialogue at the beginning of therapy when building a supportive environment is the pre-paratory focus. For example, when the client is deflecting or is entirely content focused, it is the therapist's responsibility to hold a *dialogic attitude*. At these times the therapist needs to be present with the client and imagine their reality (whilst being open to these imaginings being inaccurate). Such a dialogic attitude and commitment to dialogue is an on-going process that is built and maintained in the ground of the relationship.

My situation, my field, my lifespace is my dialogue with my world. I am committed to such dialogue for any lack of commit-ment will mean that I do not believe what I perceive, a fragmented state we could conceivably describe as a psychosis. Similarly there is certain madness in failing to commit to fully appreciating (not necessarily agreeing with) a client's way of viewing their world in a therapeutic relationship. What is the alternative to commit-ting to dialogue? To relate to the other as an 'it', to objectify, to rescue, to infantilize, to treat the other as something other than a fellow autonomous yet connected human being.

69

Non-exploitation

To say that the dialogic relationship should not be exploitative appears to be such an obvious statement that it shouldn't really need to be said. However, it clearly does need to be stated as exploitation of all kinds happens in and out of awareness by both well-intentioned therapists and knowingly manipulative exploiters (Yontef, 1981). Any movement the therapist makes away from the dialogue being in the service of the client towards being in the service of the therapist can be a form of exploitation. That is not to say that the therapist cannot receive confirmation and experience inclusion in their dialogue with the client but this should be as a by-product of the dialogic relationship.

The therapeutic relationship is unequal in terms of power. The therapist is in a more powerful position and needs to recognize their potential for abusing this power. If we consider common dynamics that emerge during the course of therapy such as the client idealizing the therapist, it becomes all too evident how such a situation could be manipulated to the advantage of the therapist whether in or out of awareness. To help the therapist understand the potential of their exploitative powers, they have a duty to explore such possibilities in their supervision and own personal therapy. They also need to consider whether they are sufficiently supported in their own life, to counter the possibility of any proactive compensatory behaviour in the therapist-client relationship. Sometimes, and with caution, physical contact is indicated in therapy (see Point 93), but this is open to abuse. If offering physical contact to a client, be certain whom you are offering it for – the client or yourself.

Acknowledging one's potential to exploit can reduce the risk of exploitation being enacted. With this in mind I would like to invite the reader to complete the following exercise as a possible exploration of their shadow qualities:

Experiential exercise
Follow the directions for the exercise covered in Point 18 but this time identify an 'anti-hero' with qualities you dislike, despise or hate. As in the earlier exercise I am not suggesting that these qualities or abilities are present in you but once you have written down the qualities consider how they might fit for you in terms of a capacity rather than enacting the quality. Now, to remain true to a field perspective, consider how these qualities can be useful in your field of experience – and in your client work.

A dialogic approach is marked by intimacy with the potential for the client to feel fully attuned to and understood. Hence, a dialogic relationship provides the maximum opportunity for the healing of past relational ruptures. It also presents the possibility of the sort of exploitation that can shatter trust.

We need to consider the cultural ground upon which the therapeutic relationship stands and how this influences the meeting in terms of potential exploitation. Are we to assume, for example, that if I face someone from a race whose ancestors were servants or slaves to my race that will not affect our meeting in the present? To do so could create a comfortable blind spot in the relationship's historical field. If we are to be true to our belief in an openness to dialogue we need to honour such relational patterns. If exploitation is present in the field, I believe that it needs to be acknowledged.

70

Living the relationship

When we wake up each morning we face a fresh new day in which pretty much anything can happen. The fact that usually the day takes a famaliar path can blind us to the small nuances in our day. We can deaden ourselves to these differences with fixed patterns in which only inconveniences stand out. Our contact boundaries harden and are less open to the novel[16]. We can numb ourselves to the aliveness of the relationships around us.

Living the relationship is not 'talking about'; it takes place in the here and now, being characterized by present-focused relating, and the therapist needs to take the lead and model such relating. To live the relationship we need to soften our contact boundary to allow us to be touched by the client. This softening is a necessary movement in order to build the ground for the possible emergence of I–Thou relating, but it can feel risky. In surrendering to the between, we can feel that there is the danger that our boundaries will permanently and completely dissolve. Such a surrender will take us through a symbolic death that is needed to allow the space for a symbolic rebirth (Jacobs, 1995). We give up our self image to contact our emergent self in this relationship here and now, an emergent self that will materialize differently in every relationship we encounter and can only be known in the meeting.

Our theoretical constructs need to remain background in the immediacy of the lived relationship with our clients. Concepts and constructs need to fall away as we open ourselves to experiencing the other. When I am living the relationship with my client and their situation, I am creating the ground for what Buber (1958) called the 'noetic' world, a world of validity, presence and being.

---

[16] As I was writing this section a confused chaffinch was tapping on the windowpane in our lounge. This chaffinch had encountered the novel in its world – this stuff we know as glass. It just couldn't work out why it could not move forwards.

Denham-Vaughan (2005) discusses the dialectic of 'will' and 'grace' present in any living relationship. This relates to the therapist needing to 'do whilst being' and 'be whilst doing'. She describes 'will' as directed action or taking the initiative, and 'grace' as receptivity and surrender. As therapists we need to be wilfully active in our being, to reach out to the client whilst balancing this act of will with allowing sufficient space for the client to reach across the relational divide where we are available to receive them grace-fully.

In a living relationship the therapist and client are not seen as separate entities but together they form a dialogic act of creation; what arises in the relationship is explored within that relationship rather than some external cause being sought. Let me give an example. In a session a client shares that she has often felt missed in the past. Now the therapist could explore where this has happened, by whom, what the feeling of being missed is like for them, all of which may have their place at certain points in the journey. However, if the therapist and client are to live the relationship as a present adventure, the therapist needs to focus on what happens in the between of *this* relationship. Interventions may then take the form of, 'How do I miss you?' or a response that offers the possibility of greater immediacy such as a self-disclosure of how the therapist is impacted, or a hunch about how they may have missed the client. Initially many clients respond with a deflection to such interventions. However, by persisting we are able to explore relational patterns that emerge in the living relationship that have the potential to bring about fundamental changes in the client's world of relationships.

71

Attunement

I recall working with a young man who was abusing alcohol to a staggering degree. In our first session he gave an account of never having been accepted by his parents, no matter what he *did*. Having sought and failed to gain some form of 'behavioural confirmation' from his parents he then sought it from his peers, 'I realized I was good at drinking, so I drank and kept drinking'. I felt profoundly sad and simply replied, 'but you still didn't really get seen, did you?' He looked surprised initially before crumpling into tears. This is one example of affect attunement where the therapist tunes into the client's emotional landscape. Affect attunement needs to be repeated across feeling states over time with particular attention to those areas that were developmentally neglected.

Attunement to the client's being-in-the-world facilitates engagement, a prerequisite for any self-development. It is central in the process of practising inclusion and is an embodied experience. In the above example I did not feel my sadness in one part of my body or just think it, rather it had the sensation of a wave of grief. You will have your style of attuning and this will shift from one person and one situation to another. We need to hold in our awareness the possibility of 'attuning' to an element of our own field of experience through a proactive counter-transference that may move us away from the client's field of relations and towards our own. However, such a misattunement – once unpicked in the therapist's supervision – should not be hastily dismissed. If viewed through a lens of co-transference (see Point 36) it could provide valuable information when we consider the point at which the therapeutic rupture occurred and offer possible insight into what past relational ruptures *may* have been like for the client. We need to track the times when we are unsuccessful in our attempts to attune with clients as well as when we appear to succeed and consider these in a wider context than the therapy dyad or group. Such occurrences need to be viewed as field events. Useful self-supervision questions could be: What pattern could be replaying?

Has the client been missed in a similar way before? What feeling states do I find easier to attune to with this client and is this a familiar pattern for me as a therapist?

There are some experimental techniques that can help the therapist in attuning to what a client *might* be experiencing. One such experiment is to assume a similar posture to the client, to 'try on' their way of sitting and/or moving. As with any experiment we need to prepare the ground (see Point 47) and be attentive to the possible exposing nature and shaming potential of the experiment. The therapist can mirror the way the client holds their body, the way in which they move and breathe noting and feeding back any areas of tension or particular sensations that arise. We need to be aware of our own habitual ways of holding our bodies and to be careful not to be telling the client what they feel, but to tentatively share what awareness arises and see if this has any resonance for the client. For example, having taken on an impression of the client's posture the therapist may share that they feel tension or awkwardness in one particular area or have a sense of making themselves small or hunched. Alternatively the therapist could walk as the client walks into the room and again describe their impressions. As always such experiments need to emerge from the dialogue and are initially a move away from immediacy into I–It relating, but can be a facilitative part of forming the ground for greater immediacy.

We need to hold in our awareness that there are different cultural meanings to behaviours. Classic examples of cultural misattunement are built upon the ground of faulty assumptions around the meaning of personal space, eye contact and bodily movements, the meaning of which can differ radically from culture to culture. To counter such assumptions we need to gain a felt sense of the client's experience through being attentive to our sensations and bodily reactions in relation to the client but also take responsibility for educating ourselves about cultural difference outside the therapy room.

Affect attunement is the recognition of the other's needs, and moving to respond to those needs. It is a step towards dialogue but not the destination. In on-going therapy we need to constantly re-attune to clients in order to be able to move towards and maintain a dialogic relationship.

72

The I–Thou attitude, the I–Thou moment

I–Thou moments are often seen as peak moments in therapy, but nurturing the possibility of these moments arising often involves a much lengthier process of the therapist maintaining a dialogic or I–Thou *attitude*. Such a relational attitude is at the heart of gestalt therapy and is characterized by a desire to genuinely meet with the other with openness, respect, acceptance and presence in a fluidly inclusive way. The I–Thou attitude makes the I–Thou moment possible. A dialogic or I–Thou attitude, the terms are used interchangeably, will include a rhythmic interchange between I–It and I–Thou relating. At times we need to step outside the therapeutic relationship to review progress and gain an overview of the relational dynamics – this requires I–It relating.

Jacobs distinguishes between the I–Thou *moment* and the I–Thou *process*. The I–Thou moment she defines as, 'a special moment of illuminated meeting wherein the participants confirm each other as the unique being each is' (1995: 54), we are absorbed with the other and the other is absorbed with us. Buber's *I and Thou* focuses almost exclusively on this intense moment of mutual contact.[17] The I–Thou process is a relational attitude that has been referred to as the dialogical (Hycner, 1985; Yontef, 1993). It is the fertile ground from which I–Thou moments *may* emerge if, and only if, this is what the client calls for. This last point is important: as described earlier, the I–Thou moment holds some of the terrors of the impasse and fear of what it might feel like standing on the edge of a relational precipice needs to be respected.

I believe that holding an I–Thou attitude with clients holds a greater importance than the I–Thou moment itself as without such an attitude the I–Thou moment can never emerge.

---

[17] In Buber's later work he diversified in his thinking and paid more attention to the I–Thou process or dialogic process. For the interested reader see Buber 1965a, 1965b, 1973.

Irrespective of whether I–Thou moments emerge or not, holding an I–Thou attitude is healing in itself. Confirmation can be achieved in such a relationship that endures over time. In holding such an attitude of equality we attend to the ground of the therapeutic relationship with an honesty and openness, without judging the client's way of being, and do so with an on-going consistency. Our honesty and openness needs to be in the service of the dialogue, rather than being, an indiscriminate sharing of whatever reactions arise for the therapist. Sadly indiscriminate self-disclosure from narcissistically-oriented therapists showing a lack of attention to the developmental phase of the therapeutic relationship has been present in the history of gestalt. Thankfully a greater emphasis upon dialogue with an appreciation of the other's phenomenology and their field has greatly reduced such practice.

A danger with focusing on the concept of I–Thou relating is that the background of the 'I' and the background of the 'Thou' can become diminished. Within the dialogic relationship we need to hold in our awareness that there are a whole field of relations 'out there' in the client's and the therapist's respective situations that impact the way contact is made 'in here'. Any dialogic relationship that takes place does so as part of both parties' lifespace, it is not an encapsulated event. We are in a situation where two lifespaces meet, with the emphasis on the client's lifespace. If we fail to attend to the client's lifespace, we see them as less than they are and consequently render true I–Thou relating impossible.

73

Self-disclosure

Self-disclosure covers an enormous area in therapy – well beyond the scope of this single point. Whether we self-disclose as therapists is not a choice, the choice is how much we self-disclose. The way we hold ourselves, the intonations in our speech, the clothes we wear and the colour of our therapy rooms are a few examples of how we will reveal something of ourselves. It is not possible to create a blank screen, nor would it be desirable in gestalt therapy.

Having evolved from psychoanalysis gestalt rebelled against the neutrality and abstinence practised in that approach. Therapist self-disclosure and the therapist's presence as a therapeutic tool entered the therapy space. This therapeutic stance opens up new possibilities for dialogue and inclusion but it is double-edged as it also opens up a greater scope for the therapist to abuse their power.

When do we self-disclose as therapists? A broad and far-reaching question with a simple answer – it all depends! In essence, we self-disclose when it is in the service of the dialogue and do not usually self-disclose when it will move the prime relational focus away from the client. 'Dialogically minded therapists discriminate and modulate their own self-disclosure in terms of what they believe will further (or truncate) the contact' (Resnick, 1995: 4). We move away from being dialogic when we develop fixed ways of being out of relation with the person before us. We need to keep our contact boundaries permeable enough to meet the demands of the situation and our therapeutic boundaries tight enough to guard against our capacity to exploit. To expand upon the answer to when to self-disclose, it all depends on the field conditions, some of which are: the developmental phase of the relationship, the client and therapist's style of relating, whether contra-indications to self-disclosure are present such as the client having suffered an acute trauma. Self-disclosure can be used positively as: validation of the client, a dialogic experiment, a challenge, a flattening of the hierarchy, a means to communicate understanding of the client's experience.

There are many different types of self-disclosure, many non-verbal. I can tell my wife that I love her and I can show my wife that I love her – I can also show my wife that I love her in my telling. The way in which we self-disclose needs to model a healthy style of relating that is direct yet respectful. We have probably all encountered the sort of pseudo self-disclosure that has more in common with blame, such as 'You make me feel angry'. Using 'I' language not only counters deflection, it can make the 'Thou' more visible. Conversely, ill-timed self-disclosure can distract from the client's developing figure.

Different types of self-disclosure can be related to the different time zones outlined by Yontef (see Point 33). We may model spontaneity by sharing a here and now reaction – a feeling, thought, sensation. Or we might share an imagining of, for example, what it might have been like for the client in their situation or of some potential we see. We might reflect on our own past experience, not through self-indulgence but to perhaps normalize the client's experience. A client I saw had a mother who was diagnosed with schizophrenia. She was profoundly concerned that she was developing the disorder because she was talking to herself; she was genuinely amazed when I disclosed that I often talked to myself out loud. Such self-disclosure can offer the client support for their on-going self-regulation.

Laura Perls gave the following broad guideline in relation to self-disclosure, 'I share verbally only that much of my awareness that will enable him to take the next step on his own – that will expand his support for taking a risk in the context of his present malfunction' (L. Perls, 1992: 119). Although I agree with Perls' philosophy, there are wider issues to consider as she is only addressing one pole of the relationship. Sometimes self-disclosure may be indicated if something that may have occurred outside the therapy room is so pressing for the therapist that it interferes with their ability to be present with the client, or that the client picks up on the reaction to this outside interference but has a pattern of self-blame. Again we cannot have a catch all approach; sometimes the therapist may need to retroflect at these times, due to the developmental stage of the relationship or the characterological style of the client's relating. We do need to be aware that reactions that are not shared are still present in the relational field and will shape the relationship.

I suggest that you consider what your growing edge may be in relation to self-disclosure. Is it to develop an ability to withhold or to be more open and how does it vary in different relationships?

74

Language

Although we are all individuals with different phenomenal worlds, we are all more alike than not, with part of our alikeness being our dependence upon language to communicate experience. The way we use language is a manifestation of ourselves, a revelation of our intimate being and our connectedness to the world and our fellow humans. Everything the gestalt therapist does is a relational event and is therefore done in accordance with dialogic principles. In the execution of these principles we use language; perhaps this is what Heidegger (1962) was referring to when he described language as the 'house of being'.

Fritz Perls invited a greater awareness of the use of language with clients, introducing the concept of holism in his search for an improvement to the psychoanalytic approach. He recognized that we attempt 'to do the impossible: to integrate personalities with the help of non-integrative language' (Perls, 1948: 567). Splits and separations play out in our use of language and are perhaps necessary for clarification but there is a danger that this can lead to the creation of false dichotomies. For instance, in naming our approach 'psycho' therapy it suggests that we are not part of a unified field, but 'that disturbance is located inside the psychic, mental apparatus of a person' (Wollants, 2008: 27).

Use of metaphor can create a dialogic bridge between us through which a level of understanding can be gained that transcends the words used (see Point 48). Spanuolo-Lobb (2002) observes that our use of language can illuminate the client's contacting style. She gives the example of a client using metaphor, saying that 'the air is heavy' indicating that the client is speaking from the experience of his body. In the language of the gestalt theory of self, this indicates id functioning. Whilst we might relate to 'the air is heavy' due to sharing a similar experience, if we meet with another who has a way of expressing themselves through language that falls outside the realms of our experience this may be a different proposition. If a client says that spiders are crawling across their skin this can also be conceptualized as verbalizing an id function, yet further exploration of this vividly described sensation can be closed if in our attempts to make sense of this awareness we categorize it as a delusion without attuning to the client. We need to creatively adapt to the client's use of language, and the further their use of language is away from our experience of the world the greater the creative adaption required. I agree with Spanuolo-Lobb (2002) that a client who expresses herself in the way described above is relating in a completely different way from someone who says, 'I'll never be able to get what I want from life.' The former is relating from their id function whereas the latter is relating from their personality function (see Point 7). Language that speaks from the id function needs to be met with an embodied language whereas language of the style of the second example (personality function) calls for the language, 'which springs from role experience, from unrealized ideals and a desire to be appreciated for the good that she has achieved' (ibid: 8).

As an attempt to accurately and completely describe our experience language must virtually always fall short. Can I ever *really* describe what my experience of my lifespace is like? I speculate that on the occasions our language assists us to move as close as possible to knowing the other, then those are the moments of I–Thou relating.

When I have a felt sense for the meaning behind your words, and you see that I have that felt sense, then for perhaps just a few fleeting moments we truly know one another.

As previously mentioned Stern (1998) discussed the loss of expression involved as language develops in infancy. As we collect our vocabulary through the years, words can replace experience rather than describe it. I believe that the more subjective forms of language move us back to a more experience-near form of description, but let us also be mindful that the meaning of language is not fixed but is a function of the interaction between the speaker and the spoken to and that function will change.

75

Rupture and repair

There is an ancient Persian curse that reads, 'May your every desire be immediately fulfilled.' We could apply this to the thera- peutic relationship because all relationships need traumas and ruptures as well as positive experiences for them to flourish and grow.

Many trainee therapists can paralyse themselves for fear of 'saying the wrong thing' when working with clients. I am touched by the care implicit in such fear, but what can be missed is that 'saying the wrong thing' is not the end of the story. Within a dialogic relationship we are not going to attune perfectly with our clients all the time, there will be relational ruptures. The meaning of contact is 'approach toward an assimilable novelty' (PHG, 1951). When we are approaching the novel in meeting the other, it is inevitable that there will be some uncertainty, excitement and/or anxiety. We might have our theories and maps to guide us but in every new inter-human meeting we are journeying into unknown territory and are likely to take a few 'wrong' turns. Being vigilant in attending to our habitual ways of moderating contact will reduce the occasions that those moderations play out with our clients but our task as therapists is not the impossible one of eliminating all slight misattunements. It is to notice that they occur and to let the client know that we notice. It is in the repairing of the misattunement and subsequent re-attunement that healing takes place.

I can attempt to explain a rupture and repair cycle but cannot hope to illustrate the process as well as any healthy mother–infant relationship. Observe such a relationship and you will notice a series of slight misattunements followed by re-attunement or to put it another way a series of relational ruptures and repairs. In the repair process an inter-personal bridge is rebuilt as healthy contact is restored and any shame or related affects experienced at the time of the rupture are experienced as a tolerable emotional state that can be regulated rather than a damning indictment on the child's way of being. The child also learns in an embodied way that ruptured interactions are repairable. Conversely, when the rupture repeatedly goes by unacknowledged or the child is chastized for it, the situational rupture is internalized. Perhaps years later that child, now an adult, might walk through the door of our therapy room as a result of experiencing this rupture in their field that has led to a disconnection from their field. Our task is to transform such out-of-awareness disconnection into the experience of connection with their current field. Part of how we might achieve this is through the owning, acknowledging and maybe apologizing for the relational ruptures that occur in the between in the here and now of the therapeutic relationship. If the therapist is vigilant and committed to this process of repair, over time together with the client they build the ground for the potential healing of toxic shame and the torn fibres of past relational being.

If we widen our view of relational ruptures from a dyadic relationship, we may gain an appreciation of the cultural impact an individualistic society can have upon the internalization of such affects as shame. Wheeler (2000) discusses such a cultural way of being in depth and how this can lead to a 'rupture in the field of belonging' arguing that repair and reconnection can be achieved through the gestalt way of holism, belonging and care.

Part 4

BECOMING: TRANSITIONS ALONG THE JOURNEY

76

Aggressing on the environment

Just consider the word 'aggression' for a few moments. What images does this word evoke? Rampaging hooligans, hostile enemies, war, attack? The first words that come up for both meanings and synonyms on my computer are 'violence' followed by 'attack' and 'hostility'. Now prefix it with 'healthy', healthy aggression – is this a contradiction in terms? Chew it over for a few moments.

PHG acknowledge the word 'aggression' has usually used to describe an unprovoked attack but its broader meaning, the way it is used in gestalt includes 'everything that an organism does to initiate contact with its environment' (1951: 70). Aggression is necessary in the contacting process to destructure in order to assimilate; liberating healthy aggression frees the individual to live creatively and spontaneously. Through healthy aggression we mobilize and organize our energy to act on our field to satisfy our emerging need. We need aggression to maintain a healthy flow in relation to our situation, to take in from our environment when needed and to armour ourselves when field conditions indicate a need for self-protection. To avoid what is toxic, unhealthy or unwelcome in the environment often takes an act of aggression. The child that does not want to eat clamps her jaw shut or spits the food out, the adult 'spits out' the unreasonable request from the other. When a healthily aggressive response is unsupported by the environment, our ability to creatively adjust may on the one hand lead to our contact boundary becoming less permeable or alter-natively the creative adjustment can lead to an adaption to avoid conflict through confluence.

Fritz Perls drew parallels with our ability to dentally aggress and the way in which we take in information, arguing that a similar destructuring process needs to take place in the assimilation of psychological 'food' as in the assimilation of actual food. The following exercise is adapted from PHG and is designed to counter introjection:

Experiential exercise
Take a single paragraph from a difficult theory book, analyse it, dissect it, really chew it over. Consider each phrase, each word and critically take it apart. Decide what the meanings of these words are for you. What sense do you make of the parts you struggle to understand? Do you retroflect (aggress on yourself) at those points by telling yourself that you are not intelligent? It may be that the author is not understandable.

The gestalt therapist Isadore From described aggression positively as a beneficial, creative and self-expressive power and argued that the aggression that led to hostility, power hungry behaviour and all kinds of acts of war did not originate in the freely spontaneous aggression discussed in gestalt theory. He saw this stemming from a bottled up aggression or a fear of impotence that leads to a craving for power and control (Miller, 1994).

Aggressing on my world is a unique aesthetic formulation of a whole that involves contact, awareness, attention, and the process of figure formation from the ground of my experience. A gestalt arises out of emergent needs and is mobilized by my ability to engage my aggressive energy. Conceptualizing this process using the gestalt cycle, my aggression moves me into action on to final contact and onwards to complete the cycle with satisfaction. I aggress on my environment just as my environment aggresses on me. Unfortunately some of the unhealthy ways we aggress on our environment (and consequently ourselves), as we are now beginning to acknowledge, do hold more of a war-like quality than is the case with healthy aggression.

77

Developmental theory

From a gestalt field perspective development is seen as situational, it is not just the person that will develop, but also the person in relation to their environment *and* their environment in relation to the person. Such a reciprocal process takes place between individual and environment rather than within the individual. A common criticism of gestalt is that it does not possess an adequate developmental theory. I believe this criticism stems from a search for a developmental theory based on our dominant cultural world-view of individualism. As already outlined gestalt does not see the individual as separate from the environment. Within gestalt lies a rich developmental theory grounded in field theory that embraces the need for the individual to constantly creatively adjust to their environment from birth to the grave.

Clients usually come to therapy when there has been a breakdown in their familiar ways of creatively adjusting in response to changed field conditions. The old strategies just aren't working due to a developmental arrest in the person-world interaction that has lost fluidity and is now out of step. The therapeutic task is to free this frozen development. To create a field where transformation is possible, we need to gain an understanding of the original field conditions to appreciate how this past field creates the client's current *phenomenal field*. For example, the client may have been brought up in a dangerous household and now perceives the world as dangerous. This client may then creatively adjust to their current situation as they did in their past situation. This way of being has become a habit, a fixed gestalt.

> Developmentally, we could say that the structure of the interactive field of childhood, *becomes the structure of the person's inner world.*
>
> (Wheeler, 2000: 257, original italics)

An often-cited Fritz Perls' (1973) quote that views development as a movement from environmental support to self-support is not representative of most gestalt therapist's views on healthy development. Laura Perls' (1992) view that development is only possible if there is sufficient environmental support is far more representative. Developmental ruptures occur when there is a lack of support from the environment. This may manifest physically in, say, a parent consistently failing to support the infant's head sufficiently or psychologically in a child being consistently ridiculed. Whether the environment's failure to provide sufficient support is physical or psychological it will affect the person's physical and psychological development. The unsupported infant may not allow herself to be held physically or psychologically when they become an adult.

Development is not a linear process. We do not wave goodbye to a developmental task and simply move on; the completion of that development task recedes into our ground and becomes a part of us. We need to re-visit and re-assess old creative adjustments that may have become fixed gestalts. In this respect Daniel Stern's work fits well with a gestalt philosophy. His thinking, particularly regarding what he refers to as domains of relatedness (Stern, 1998), will be of interest to those wanting to complement gestalt's non-linear developmental theory. Like gestalt therapists Stern sees development in a relational context and as inherently inter-subjective, 'Our minds are not separate or isolated, and we are not the only owners of our own mind' (Stern, 2003: 23).

A human being's development is a function of the field over time, a field that is always in a state of flux. In gestalt we do not focus solely on the early years of development but consider it over a lifetime. The need to develop for an elderly person in adapting to a rapidly shrinking world in terms of their physical ability may be just as acute as the needs and struggles of an infant or child dealing with a rapidly expanding world. Whereas the lifespace of a child is constantly expanding, the physical lifespace of an elderly person is characterized by shrinkage, yet the elderly person's lifespace can continue to expand in terms of creative interactions with their environment (Wollants, 2008). A difference on this developmental journey is that in our third age we are also aware of what we have lost, whereas in infancy we are on a constant voyage of discovery. In gestalt we see the person as an extension of his situation. I would like to close this point with the words of one of gestalt's elder statesmen:

> Autonomous statements of self begin with temperament at birth and throughout the life span the person is developing an increasing capacity to articulate self and to define and declare her or his particularity. Autonomy and identity formation are life-long processes, and we become increasingly skilled at them the longer we live.
>
> (Lichtenberg, 1991: 35)

78

The five layer model

Fritz Perls developed the 'five layer model of neurosis' towards the end of his career. Having first presented the model in one of his four lectures given in 1966 (Fagan and Shepherd, 1971), he altered his thinking about the layers[18] with his later model outlining the levels of neurotic disturbances covered below (Perls, 1969). This later model is the one that is usually quoted and it takes the form of 'peeling an onion' on the way to the central 'layer' of authenticity. The five layers are described as follows:

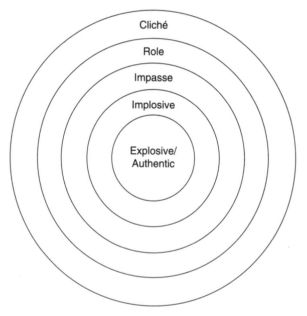

Figure 4.1

---

[18] Originally, Perls identified the five layers as: the phoney layer, the phobic layer, the impasse, the implosive state and the explosion.

1. *The Cliché layer* – This is the level of ordinary social chitchat. Cultural norms may be followed in a programmed way. Examples of this superficial level of relating are talking about the weather or a greeting of 'how are you?' with no real interest in the true reply, which may generally be a clichéd 'oh, fine'.

2. *The Role or Role-playing layer* – As the name suggests the individual functions in role. The person acts and adapts to the role whether that be the 'tough' manager, the 'vulnerable' client or the 'caring' therapist. If this type of relating persists, people can become role-locked into this inauthentic way of being.

3. *The Impasse layer* – This is marked by stuckness. In the impasse layer there is an internal conflict between staying with the impasse and moving back to the relative comfort of living through roles and clichés. Characterized by existential angst and confusion the therapist needs to support the client in staying with the unknown in the faith that something will emerge from the client's internal conflict.

4. *The Implosive layer* – Sometimes referred to as the death layer. The client needs to make an authentic choice, but there are so many choices that will all move the client in different directions. Their muscles pull and push in different directions. In the face of these opposing choices the client is paralysed. It might be tempting here for the therapist to offer some direction but to do so could rob the client of the opportunity to discover their authentic 'core'.

5. *Explosion/Authentic layer* – This is where the client contacts their authentic self. Perls identified four types of explosion, '. . . explosion into joy, into grief, into orgasm, into anger' (Fagan and Shepherd, 1971: 22).

Criticisms of the five-layer model are that it is inconsistent with Perls' earlier collaborative work in PHG (1951) in that it suggests a model based on a core self rather than the model of self as process discussed in PHG. Consequently, I question whether the model is sufficiently appreciative of field dynamics in that it promotes an individualized view of the client and I-It relating. These may be some of the reasons why it has, 'fallen into disfavour and disuse, and is generally seen as having little bearing on the theory and practice of modern Gestalt Therapy' (Philippson, 2002). However, this has not stopped Philippson applying the model in his work, viewing it as having a good fit with gestalt's existential stance and perceiving it as being close to Goodman's description of the therapeutic process in PHG. Part of the beauty of gestalt is the way different practitioners integrate different concepts. This does make it a difficult approach to learn – there is no gestalt manual. As individuals pursuing a common cause we develop our individual philosophies based on who we are – our authentic self!

79

Experimentation

> The true method of knowledge is experiment.
>
> William Blake (1977)

As discussed in previous points responsible creative experimentation that emerges from the therapeutic dialogue is one of the cornerstones of gestalt (see Points 45 and 47). The limits of the range of experiments available to us as therapists are defined by the limits of our creativity coupled with field constraints including ethical considerations such as the need for therapeutic boundaries. Philippson (2001: 160) discusses three experimental methods: enactment with awareness, exaggeration and reversal. I have borrowed this format below to demonstrate these methods.[19] These three 'families' of experimental methods can form different phases of the same experiment as demonstrated below. Such an experiment might begin with the client identifying a quality or trait that is being 'partially projected' (Perls, 1969). We might work to heighten awareness through enacting thus:

Client – You are such a powerful person.

Therapist – What are you aware of in your body as you say this to me? I suggest you repeat that slowly and just pay attention to what is happening in your body.

Client – (*having repeated the initial sentence*). My stomach is turning, I feel transparent. I want to back away from you.

Therapist – How about just playing with that and backing away from me?

Client – *(moves back in the chair and then moves the chair back)* Hmm, now I feel that you're messing me around – moving me backwards and forwards. I feel a bit cross.

---

[19] With thanks to Peter Philippson for his kind permission.

There are many choice points in experiments. Here the therapist could focus on the client's experience of 'being moved' backwards and forwards (when he actually chose to do so himself) or to explore his 'feeling cross'. Such choice points often present and the direction of the therapy is likely to be decided by what possible growing edges may have surfaced in the ground of the therapeutic relationship to date and how safe an emergency has been created (see Point 45). This client has a background of experiencing difficulty with assertion and expressing anger.

We now move into inviting exaggeration.

Therapist – A bit cross? *(pauses)* Try breathing out, and then into your stomach and see if you contact any more of that feeling *(therapist models by putting her hand on her stomach and breathing 'into it')*.

Client – *(having exhaled and inhaled a few times)*. I guess I do feel more than a bit cross with you.

Therapist – I'd like to invite you to speak from that 'cross place' and make a direct statement to me about what you'd like.

(The client may well need to be supported in exaggerating his response, but due to lack of space we'll assume that support has been given.)

Client – Quit telling me what to do! You sound just like my mother, do this, do that – I'll do just as I like!

In a reversal the client would then be invited to take the part of the other.

Therapist – Would you like to experiment with being your mother? Try changing places and talk as if you were her. See what emerges.

(It is important in such a reversal that the client does not remain in the same seat as this could lead to boundary confusion.)

Client – *(expresses with energy)* No! I don't want to. Quit telling me what to do.

Therapist – Okay, I have no desire to tell you what to do. I can really see and hear your power and am really impacted by you. Wow, you're powerful.

Client – *(Looks visibly moved, eyes water)* This feels different.

This reversal facilitated a different and more immediate turn as the client asserted his authority. It is important to stay with the underlying process, the reason for the experiment, rather than missing the client by following a format. The function of a gestalt experiment is to heighten awareness of *what is*. It may then lead to alternatives of what could be but not what should be. The example of an experiment given here is a highly graded experiment. In grading experiments we need to consider the dialectic of strangeness/familiarity and manage this in such a way as to sustain energy at the contact boundary. Grading experiments too highly by venturing too far along the continuum of the ego-alien will result in withdrawal and can shame the client.

I have found that some of the most effective gestalt experiments are the simplest. A client who arrives complaining of suffering from anxiety and panic attacks rushes in. His breathing is rapid as he hurries to give several examples of how he has been affected. The therapist may invite him to stop and breathe, but if she paid close attention to when the client changes subjects she would notice that he does not breathe out at these points. Contact with the environment does not only involve inspiration but also expiration. Breathing out can give a person a sense of closure or completion. Physiologically symptoms associated with anxiety will increase along with an increased intake of oxygen. Therefore attending only to breathing inwards with a 'take a breath' intervention could increase anxiety.

An experiment is an exploration of the client's relationship with their phenomenal world, a method of exploring what is pressing in on the client's situation. 'It is used to expand the range of the individual, showing him how he can extend his habitual sense of boundary where emergency and excitement exist' (Polster and Polster, 1973: 112). No gestalt experiment is designed to have a particular outcome. By definition an experiment moves the therapeutic relationship into I-It relating, therefore the therapist needs to take responsibility for maintaining an I-Thou attitude. An experiment is a technique and although we use techniques to help facilitate awareness in gestalt, we are not technique based. 'Technique needs to be based in the *relationship* between person and person' (Hycner, 1993: 4).

80

Developing supports

When I was first asked to write this book I was excited but also found the prospect daunting. What support would I need? Two established gestalt writers freely offered their expertise[20] and I bought that new laptop I'd been promising myself. In writing the first few pages I became overly technical through a need to impress. A way around this, suggested by a friend and colleague, was to assemble a review team of gestalt trainees to offer feedback on the clarity of my writing. I contacted four such individuals who gave useful feedback. As the project progressed my needs changed. Contacting the review team became more of a bind than a support. One meeting with each of the established authors gave me sufficient material and ideas regarding structure and direction. I began to withdraw from this form of interpersonal support and got on with the task in hand. My support needs focused more on activities that got me more in contact with my body – exercise and playing a musical instrument helped me free the inevitable writing blocks. The sedimented supportive relationships from my past and present – my parents, brothers, Karin my wife, an old English teacher from my schooldays – may not have always been figural but they were certainly part of the solid ground I stood upon with the more recent additions to that ground from 'the gestalt world'.

As I look back on this process I would conceptualize it by saying that I developed supports in the present from the ground of support in my past and was fluid in changing my supports in response to my emerging needs (self in process). My awareness of existing supports was heightened through dialogue with others and I manipulated elements of my field to fulfil a supportive function for the demands of my situation. I acknowledge that I am fortunate in having a background of supportive relationships,

---

[20] Sally Denham-Vaughan and Malcolm Parlett both kindly offered free consultations and support in writing this book.

something that many others do not have. In our work with clients such experience might need to be built, as far as is possible, in the therapeutic relationship.

Contact and support are inseparable functions of a fluid and dynamic process. As illustrated above support needs change and needs to be met with different types of contact from the field at different points in a journey. Just as we cannot separate figure from ground in gestalt, neither can we separate support from contact. If we are not in good contact we will not be able to engage fully with the support available, and support is the ground that makes good contact possible. Support is 'everything that facilitates the on-going assimilation and integration of experience for a person, relationship or society' (L. Perls, 1992). When there is a lack of support from the environment, contact is muted or minimized in the creative adjustment to the unsupportive situation. If this is an enduring situation, as say in the family home in childhood or the person's cultural field, then the creative adjustment hardens into a fixed gestalt. As PHG state the organism assimilates 'from the environment what it needs for its very growth' (1951: viii). Environments vary greatly in the growthful material they contain.

The client who faces us with a problem in relation to their current situation will have a history of organismically self-regulating in order to gain the best possible outcome earlier in their lives. The Paradoxical Theory of Change (see Point 23) illustrates gestalt's philosophical belief that we cannot bring about change by aiming directly for it. As therapists we need to provide a supportive field for the client to begin to acknowledge and move towards accepting *what is now*. We explore the client's present reality, the ground conditions that support the current figure. In this exploration we need to work towards heightening the client's bodily awareness; if we are out of touch with our bodies we cannot make creative adjustments in relation to our present environment. Part of creating a supportive field for growth is to model a healthy process of maintaining and developing our own supports. We need to support ourselves as therapists to support our clients in making a movement where, through 'the between', healing is possible.

Some questions that may be helpful to ask yourself in relation to support when working with clients are:

What kind of support is needed for this relationship right now?
How can the quality of contact be increased between us?
How does this person currently support herself in the session?
How does this person support himself in his daily life?
What is 'support' for this person?
Do I feel like supporting this person right now? (Exploring possible co-transference)
What relational themes emerge between us regarding use of support?

81

Polarities and the top dog/under dog

> Excess of sorrow laughs;
> Excess of joy weeps.
>
> William Blake (1977)

The theory of polarities begins with a collection of opposing forces that may be interpersonal or intrapersonal, in or out of awareness. Every quality we possess is one end of a continuum with the opposite end of that continuum also residing within us as a potentiality. In possessing a capacity to love we also possess a capacity to hate. Although this can be denied by virtue of our mere ability to imagine the shadow quality which proves its existence. There is an old Chinese proverb, 'Fish don't know that they are wet' illustrating that contrast is needed. Light needs dark to exist just as shadow qualities are needed for their polar opposites to exist.

Polarities can apply to many different areas: to polarities of the self (Zinker, 1977), polarities of the therapy process, polarities in styles of contact (see Point 20), polarities in our cultural field. Wherever this theory is applied the same principle holds, that of yin and yang, in that the further we move into the dark the closer we move towards the light and vice versa, also that the light contains aspects of the dark and vice versa. We all limit our self-concept to a greater or lesser degree through disowning some of our human qualities and potentials.

Some examples of polarities in relation to self-concept (Zinker, 1977) are as follows:

Brilliance	Dullness
Kindness	Cruelty
Selflessness	Selfishness
Fluidity	Rigidity
Warmth/Friendliness	Coldness/Distance
Care	Ruthlessness

You can play with the polarities that fit for you in developing the above further. Some qualities may have more than one opposing quality or you may disagree with some of the opposites I have listed.

MacKewn (1997) suggested a similar set of polarities for working as a gestalt therapist. Examples of which are:

Trained	Fresh
Theoretical	Atheoretical
Simple	Complex
Empathetic	Tough
Ordered	Chaotic
Systematic	Spontaneous
Tracking present process	Bringing in other aspects of the field

Healthy functioning is achieved through extending the polarity and with it the range of the continuum between the polarities. It is between the tension of these opposites that we need to find a place to stand whilst being responsive to our changing field. In heightening our awareness by extending the continuum between polarities we create space for complete and differentiated experience.

Fritz Perls worked extensively with a particular type of polarity he identified as top dog/under dog (Perls, 1969). The top dog is the voice of what the individual *should* be doing and consequently would often contain introjected material – we could also think of it as the voice of our *will*. The under dog is more spontaneous, rebellious and impulsive. An example of this dialectic might be,

Top dog: I really must go down to the gym and get myself fit.
Under dog: To hell with that, I want to lie in the sun with a glass of wine.

You can probably see how this type of 'split' would lend itself to a two-chair gestalt experiment. In encouraging the client to enact this split with her role-playing each part, Perls would pay attention not only to what was being said in the conflict but also to the process of the dialogue, in particular how one part spoke to the other. What unfolded was usually a face-paced, dismissive self-righteousness on both sides with the therapist's task being to mediate between the two to achieve greater integration and appreciation of the other's viewpoint. The top dog dichotomy, as the name suggests, presents as the more powerful part but the under dog only hides its power behind a victim-like facade. One of Perls' trainees at the time reflects that he learnt an important lesson that, 'It takes two to resolve an issue and only one to keep resolution from happening' (Melnick, 2003: 176). This is something for us all to bear in mind in our work with conflict whether this is an internal conflict or conflict presenting in a system. Let us also be mindful that any individual with an internal conflict is experiencing a manifestation of a field event or on-going field condition.

Clients may be resistant about going into shadow qualities, preconfiguring them as unilaterally negative. I will close this point with the following thought. The writer Guy de Maupassant lived in Paris and despised the Eiffel Tower. He lunched regularly in the restaurant at the top; it was the only place that he could look out upon Paris without his view being spoilt. Who knows what the view might be from a shadow quality until we enter it?

82

'Aha' experience

An 'aha' experience is quite simply a moment of sudden insight. Often it will be preceded by a period of stuckness, an impasse, and surface as the client begins to accept that impasse or makes an authentic movement away from it. The client reconfigures their field. When this reorganization occurs a new integration of the situation falls into place as the client creatively adjusts to their field differently. Much excitement is generated as the 'aha' experience forms; everything suddenly seems to make sense in the moment of 'coming together'. The ground will have been attended to sufficiently for the formation of a strong vibrant figure to emerge. Such experiences are by no means the only ways of gaining insight and it is pointless aiming for them as they are process events that emerge between client and therapist.

There are times in therapy when relentlessly attending to the client's awareness through contact exercises and the like can obstruct the very process we are trying to facilitate. The call from the client may change to one of simply 'being with' whilst the work to date sediments down. To paraphrase Paul Goodman (1977), it is time to stand out of the way and let nature heal. At such times the therapist's unobtrusive presence can lead seemingly magically to the client integrating in one swift moment what has been experienced to date as disparate parts or fragments. This is the 'aha' experience. The real skill of the therapist is in the timing of the adjustment in their therapeutic stance, which can only be achieved through close observation of the client's phenomenology. Just as the 'aha' experience is an embodied experience, so too is the groundwork that makes this experience possible.

'Aha' experience can be facilitated through experimentation. An example might be where a client is agonizing over a decision, for example, 'Should I take that new job or not?' Rather than engage in some circular discussion about the pros and cons, the therapist might invite a two-chair experiment with one chair representing one choice and one the other. In the therapy room the client might metaphorically move to the new job (the other chair) and comment from that place. Alternatively, such insight could be facilitated with a form of enactment or other experimental techniques. Whatever the experiment, it is the minutely detailed observation from the therapist with attention to what is often taken for granted that leads to the 'aha' experience (L. Perls, 1989).

83

Catharsis and release

Catharsis is primarily concerned with undoing retroflection through facilitating an expression of tension and pent-up emotion held in the client's body. This retroflective process is invariably supported by introjected beliefs and may be reinforced by cultural ground introjects and gender stereotyping. The releasing of such material can be dramatic, loud and can involve a range of expression in experimentation: screaming, shouting, hitting cushions, expressive art and dancing. For catharsis to be of therapeutic benefit the client needs to be sufficiently well grounded in the therapeutic relationship. Due to the potentially explosive nature of catharsis the therapist needs to be vigilant in maintaining safety in any experiment where catharsis is likely. In the expression of powerful aggressive emotions such as anger, accidents can happen, clients can hurt themselves whilst enacting the experiment.

Although catharsis will often provide an emotional release it is a figural event in the therapeutic journey and should not be viewed as the ultimate goal. What lies beneath the need for catharsis is probably where the focus of further therapy lies – a need to impress, a host of introjects that restrict expression, a role-locked way of being, locked-in musculature resulting in physical problems. We need to consider catharsis as a possible step along a journey bearing in mind that it could be an unnecessary detour. Catharsis without awareness, assimilation and integration into the client's situation is of limited use. I'm not advocating that we shy away from facilitating catharsis – pyrotechnics can be wonderfully illuminating, but is the client simply left with a desire for one explosion after another? Those of you who exercise vigorously will probably be able to relate to the fact that, 'a cathartic episode can produce a temporary sense of well-being due to the release of natural opiates. This may produce a potentially misleading sense of resolution' (Joyce and Sills, 2001: 157). Such a process can be addictive and simply replay without therapeutic benefit. If we then stay with the cathartic expression we simply create and/or reinforce a fixed gestalt.

There are some styles of relating where catharsis might be a harmful intervention. For instance, people with borderline or histrionic styles of relating are already adept at moving into emotional peaks spontaneously – that might be what is causing the relational problem! With every client we meet we need to be considering what their growing edge might be at that time in relation to their situation. If someone moves into a cathartic release easily are we pushing at a growing edge? If not we need to question whether we are practising therapy. In the example given in Point 45 I imagined that Lydia could have easily moved into a confrontative way of being. I would have missed her had I proceeded in facilitating this style of cathartic work.

As therapists we need to ask ourselves what our investment is in the client 'getting into their emotion'.[21] We need to consider the value of catharsis in the light of the client's complete situation rather than simply valuing catharsis per se. If some form of explosive expression is indicated, we need to appreciate the restrictions that the current field imposes – loud dramatic expression may not go down well in a busy Health Centre! In some ways this can be a useful limitation as there are often restricting field conditions in people's lives. We can think creatively and tangentially around such issues, generating alternative forms of cathartic release.

In the 1960s and 70s many practitioners, some with only a basic knowledge of techniques, characterized gestalt by dramatic catharsis that had more in common with theatre than therapy. What developed was an anti-theoretical attitude creating what has been expressively referred to as a 'boom-boom-boom' style of therapy (Resnick, 1995; Yontef, 1993) – a figure-bound, simplistic approach that held the false promise of quick, lasting change.

If we work organically with the client and invite catharsis as it is called for in the flow of their experience, if it surfaces an emergent need, it can help facilitate lasting change and heightened awareness. What we need to question as therapists is our own

---

[21] Staemmler (2009) discusses the possibility, backed by research, that cathartic expression of anger can *increase* subsequent aggression.

biases for or against cathartic work. Where for instance does our bias stand between frustration and intensity, permissiveness and control and excitement and inhibition? (Naranjo, 1982). I cannot say that I am for or against facilitating catharsis – until I am facing a client and have built a picture of the way they relate to their situation.

84

Developing awareness of awareness

The awareness of awareness process is discussed by Yontef (1993) and relates to a wider awareness of the whole therapy situation rather than the client simply heightening their awareness of specific problem areas. As developing what Yontef refers to as 'straight-forward' awareness is the building block for the development of this more sophisticated process, let us start there – as we would with a client.

Awareness is the spontaneous sensing of what arises within you in relation to your situation. PHG describe the process of awareness poetically and differentiate it from introspection thus: 'Awareness is like a glow of coal which comes from its own combustion; what is given by introspection is like the light reflected from an object when a flashlight is turned upon it' (PHG, 1951: 75). They go on to describe that in awareness a process is happening in the total organism whereas in introspection a part of the organism is split off, similar to the process of egotism described in Point 15. This part they name the deliberate ego and describe as opinionated. Unlike this single flashlight, awareness of awareness illuminates the whole awareness process with a similar glow to that from within the coal, being free from the ties of opinionated bonds.

So what is this like in the nuts and bolts of the gestalt therapy session? Well, rather than developing awareness of the nut or the bolt, or even the nut and the bolt, awareness of the whole structure and the way in which the client puts the nut and bolt together, its function and connection to a greater whole – the construction of their awareness with all its influences – is developed. The client moves beyond the straightforward awareness of presenting issues to a reflexive awareness of their overall awareness process, 'this sophisticated phenomenological attitude leads to insight into character structure and into the pattern of avoidance of awareness' (Yontef, 1993: 251). There is an appreciation that any figural piece of work has emerged from, and will fall back into, the ground of the therapeutic relationship and the client's wider field of relationships. The dots – that were previously separate aware-ness events – are joined, with acknowledgement that the completed form is part of a larger pattern.

Yontef quotes Idhe (1977: 128) regarding *phenomenological ascent*. In this attitude there is greater clarity of perception, increased openness to viewing situations in a variety of different ways with an attuned sensitivity to one's own clarity or lack of clarity in relation to the structure of a situation. One gains a broader appreciation of the situation rather than viewing single aspects of the whole.

85

Individual and group therapy

I am a great believer in group therapy but am aware that it can mistakenly be viewed as a kind of second-class therapy that 'does not go as deep' as individual therapy. If we subscribe to this view it follows that the therapeutic process is based on a separate, individualized view of self where others dilute psychological space rather than add to it. As a gestalt philosophy sees self as 'an on-going assimilation of experience' (Philippson, 2009: 78), well facilitated group therapy can offer a wider range of experience for self-growth. The intersubjective opportunities multiply the possible areas in which such growth can take place. For this reason, and those listed below, I believe that gestalt group therapy is indicated for many clients and trainee therapists – possibly after engaging in individual therapy.

In a group setting the client learns that the world does not fall apart if they express some 'forbidden' emotion or way of being. They can gain wider feedback and a range of different perspectives from other group members as well as the facilitator. There can be an experiential learning of group dynamics and how these are co-created, for instance, how different group members may carry certain emotions or qualities 'for' the group. Such dynamics are invariably representative of what happens in the person's wider field.

The range of experimentation possible is increased. For example, the whole group can be involved in enactments such as when working with dreams or recreating situations. Clients can experiment with different ways of reaching out for support and authentic ways of being with others.

When a therapist or therapists (groups are often co-facilitated) set up a group, the fore-contact stage of the process is of great importance and can lead to problems later if not attended to. I don't intend to provide a comprehensive list of all factors that require consideration – it really all comes down to the person(s) running the group.[22] However, I believe the following are worth mentioning:

- Potential group members need to have sufficient ego strength – a strong enough sense of 'I' (and relatively consistent).
- The mix of male and female members needs to be considered.
- Members need to have an ability and a willingness to hold basic boundaries and respect others' confidentiality.
- That group members are able to function at a level where they are able to interact with others.

There are many different styles of gestalt group leadership/ facilitation. Probably the best known is the 'hot seat' model pioneered by Fritz Perls, in which group interaction was kept to a minimum and even actively discouraged. In essence, this took the form of one-to-one therapy in a group, with the group's function being to serve as a screen for the present incumbent of the hot seat's projections. The exclusion of the group's interaction limits the scope of this style of group. Perls' 'hot seat' model provided a point of departure for the development of gestalt group therapy.

Development of the gestalt group post 'hot seat'

The Polsters (1973) discuss their work with a 'floating hot seat' model that was inclusive of group interaction, allowing space for the exploration of participants' habitual ways of moderating contact. It differed from Perls 'hot seat' model markedly because the movement into a focus on a group member emerged from the group interaction rather than someone simply volunteering to work with the group leader.

Joseph Zinker (1977) placed an emphasis upon here and now on-going group experience alongside the process of developing awareness through contact between participants. He employed

---

[22] Harris (2007), an experienced gestalt group leader in the UK, when reviewing Bud Feder's book on groups (2006) noted that Feder offered prospective group members a 12-page document. Harris's preference was to offer a few ground rules and to work with what surfaced.

interactional experimentation in facilitating a sense of community within the group.

Elaine Kepner (1980) discussed three possible different foci for attention in gestalt group work: the intrapersonal, the interpersonal and the group as a whole (emerging group patterns). It follows that she was committed to working with the individual and the individual as part of a greater whole.

We can think of gestalt group facilitation in terms of a continuum with the leader-led 'hot seat' style at one end of the continuum and a totally inclusive virtually leaderless style at the other.

As with any system there is a danger that a gestalt therapy group creates an impermeable boundary around itself and thus isolates itself and its members from supports from the wider field. Relatively few accounts of gestalt group therapy relate to the group in the context of the wider field. A gestalt therapy group can be an embodiment of the whole being greater than the sum of its parts, but let us not lose sight of the fact that the gestalt therapy group is also part of a greater whole.

86

Endings

The ending of the therapeutic relationship can be an evocative event for both client and therapist, echoing back to previous endings in each of their lives. As therapists we need to develop an awareness of our patterns in ending relationships and question how these may influence endings with clients.

Experiential exercise
Sit comfortably and close your eyes noticing any areas of tension in your body. Take your time, breathe regularly out and in, and just notice whether this tension eases or remains. Now scan through a range of past relationships in your life with a focus on the way they ended. Pay attention to any changes in tension that may occur in your body or any thoughts that emerge as you picture these past relationships. What patterns do you notice? Do any of these ways of breaking contact play out in microcosm for you, for example in everyday social contact?

Whether we are working with clients long or short term the ending is part of the relationship from the beginning and needs to be acknowledged. A simple contract around ending may well suffice in the initial stages of therapy, the nature of which will vary depending on the intended length of the therapy. For clients attending short-term therapy (up to around 15 sessions) I request that we devote one complete session to an ending so that we can look at any unfinished business and any issues ending might have brought up for them. It also affords an opportunity to explore any co-transference in our ending and whether there is anything in my reaction that reflects the client's experience of their field, for instance, if I am irritated with their decision to function independently just as their parents were. With clients engaging in long-term work I make an agreement to negotiate the ending period during the course of therapy. It can be a fine balance in the initial stages of therapy between acknowledging that there will be an ending and not dampening the excitement of new contact.

If we look at the therapy journey through a phasic lens, the length of the ending phase in comparison to the beginning and middle phases of therapy will depend on a variety of factors. Two major factors are:

- The client's history of endings – for clients with a history of unsatisfactory, sudden or distressing endings this can be the most important phase of therapy, affording the opportunity for the client to experience a healthy ending process perhaps for the first time.
- The client's enduring pattern of relating – a major consideration will be the client's relational style. For a client whose relating is characterized by confluence and dependence or avoidance the ending phase of therapy might *be* the therapy. Different phases of therapy might hold greater importance for clients with other contacting styles. For example, a client who displays paranoid traits in the earlier phases of therapy is likely to present a greater challenge as they struggle to develop a level of trust.

Factors in the wider field will also impact the way in which we end. Western societal pressures leave us pretty well culturally programmed to avoid satisfaction and a process of withdrawal by rushing on to the next task. Such pressure can be mirrored in therapy training as a need to produce the next assignment can take precedence over feeling satisfaction and gradually withdrawing from the last assignment.

Ending provides the chance for assimilation and to leave the relationship without unfinished business. To help facilitate this process addressing the following areas can be useful:

- *Reminisce* over the time spent together, perhaps sharing your impressions of the client when you first met (grade this appropriately!) compared with how you experience them now. This is an opportunity for reflection on the process of therapy over time and might include changes in the client's life outside the therapy room.

- *Regrets* – An opportunity for the client to ensure that he leaves without unfinished business, it might also be appropriate for the therapist to share some of their regrets. Sharing even minor regrets, maybe unreasonable hopes or unrealistic expectations in the here and now can be enormously freeing.
- *Remember* specific incidents or change points that stand out over the course of therapy. They might be a memorable experiment that was completed or a seemingly innocuous interaction.

A two-way dialogue covering the above can run over a single session or a series of sessions.

Sometimes, usually in the early stages of therapy, a client may just stop attending sessions. This can leave the therapist with a host of possible feelings and reactions. These should be managed with the support of their supervisor and/or own personal therapy rather than provoking them to make direct contact with the client. In terms of closing the relationship with the absent client, I would suggest a brief letter expressing regret at them missing their appointment and inviting the client to make contact, including a date when you will assume they no longer wish to continue with therapy and wishing them well for the future.

87

On-going self-therapy

As therapists our aim is to put ourselves out of business – for the client to move on and build their own on-going support in relation to their situation. So what is self-therapy from a gestalt perspective? We have seen that self emerges at the contact boundary and forms in contact with the environment. In healthy relating there is a fluid flow in our ever-changing process of selfing. It follows that what is needed in on-going self-therapy is something that supports a spontaneous energetic flow between the organism and the environment.

As discussed when therapy goes well the client expands their awareness continuum and their range of support functions through an increased ability to be in contact with their present situation. During the therapeutic journey we may invite experimentation beyond the therapy room or the client may move into this spontaneously. From such experiments possible directions for on-going self-therapy can emerge. These possibilities cover a vast range but fundamentally have one thing in common – contact with the novel. This may be the novel in terms of engaging in a new activity, a different way of relating, a physical or psychological challenge, creating space, remaining in the impasses/fertile void rather than moving on to the next task.

Two examples from clients who developed their own on-going self-therapy can illustrate the process of building self-in-relation-to-environment support and the creativity inherent within the people we face. In the process both 'Mary' and 'Jody' taught me that suggesting options could limit rather than expand horizons.

Mary, a quiet and rather timid middle-aged woman, arrived for therapy experiencing debilitating levels of anxiety with panic attacks and agoraphobic type behaviour in that she avoided venturing out of her house unless absolutely necessary (encouragingly her therapy fell into this category). She had engaged well in therapy and we were nearing the end of the 12 sessions permitted by her insurance company. Her anxiety appeared to be supported by a retroflective process around her anger that she had been resistant to expressing in therapy. Given the limited period of time available we had concentrated on working with her anxiety and associated struggle in venturing out and supplemented the work with homework between sessions. We had agreed that she would visit the city centre on the Saturday prior to our penultimate session. In that session she surprised me by announcing that she had not only visited the city centre, but had met up with a friend and they had gone to a football match. It transpired that part of the function of her visiting the match was that she could 'scream and shout' at the players – undoing retroflection. She also knew that the crowd were not looking at her and therefore being with so many people only concerned her minimally. Mary went on to 'prescribe' her own self-therapy to attend these football matches regularly.

Jody was a 24-year-old whose presenting problem she described as 'low self-esteem'. She worked in a call-centre where she received a constant stream of complaints, which mirrored how she had been put down in the past. She hated the work but felt stuck as she projected her power and creativity onto others. She loved art and spent hours on the Internet scanning various artists' work, 'but I could never do anything like that' was one of her introjected beliefs. Jody disproved her own hypothesis as artwork did prove to be an open door for her expression in our therapy and with support she was able to experiment producing artwork outside our therapy sessions, although this was always done secretively. After a further year in therapy Jody was challenging her introjects about not being good enough and noticing how she projected her power and creativity onto others, she is now continuing her on-going self-therapy on an interactive arts degree at university.

Part 5

ETHICS AND VALUES: KEY SIGNPOSTS FOR ALL JOURNEYS

88

Therapeutic boundaries

Ethical behaviour emerges from an embodied ethical attitude in the world. The development and maintenance of such an attitude cannot be created through reams of ethical codes from Institutes or governing bodies. An ethical therapist lives her life ethically, she does not don some metaphorical 'ethical white coat' but is an ethical person first. Such an attitude is in itself therapeutic and from it therapeutic boundaries can be integrated into the therapist's practice. Therapeutic boundaries should emerge from an attitude of care.

Together with an ethical attitude we also need knowledge of what therapeutic boundaries are needed within the therapy relationship. In cricket a boundary is something that marks the farthest limit of the playing area, likewise a therapeutic boundary serves to contain the event that takes place within it. Boundaries hold the therapeutic relationship in place and once the therapeutic relationship ventures beyond those boundaries it becomes something other than therapy. Although the client does carry some responsibility for adhering to therapeutic boundaries it is the responsibility of the therapist to provide a safe container for the work by outlining the therapeutic boundaries and ensuring that the relationship is held within these boundaries. To provide a safe container for therapy we need to be clear around the following areas:

Confidentiality – Essential in forming and maintaining a therapeutic relationship is holding confidentiality and being clear about the limits of confidentiality. These limits relate to safety; should the client become a danger to themselves or others, confidentiality would need to be broken. The therapist also needs to take material from the session to their supervisor (see Point 94) and may wish to gain the client's permission to record sessions for this purpose. For a fuller discussion on confidentiality I suggest perusing the UKCP[23] or BACP[24] websites.

Limits of the relationship – Clients new to therapy do not always understand why we cannot meet outside the therapy space. Many clients have had experience of having had their personal boundaries crossed or violated; to meet outside therapy would cross a boundary. Although we work to equalize the therapeutic relationship, there is a very real power imbalance. This is one of the reasons that the therapeutic relationship should be limited to precisely that. Contamination can take place, even long after therapy has finished.

Sexual boundaries – To me it goes without saying that *any* sexual advance by a therapist is gross abuse of their power and that a given therapeutic boundary is that sexual feelings will not be acted upon. It might seem that this goes without saying, but sadly there are examples of such transgressions throughout the history of psychotherapy and not only our distant history. Although these individuals damage the whole profession through their actions, thankfully they represent a tiny minority amongst a group of honourable practitioners.

'Business' matters – Be clear around fees (if these apply), the length of sessions, the amount of notice required for cancellation of a session and the number of sessions you recommend should the client wish to end therapy.

Length of therapy contract – If there is a set number of sessions available, as in brief therapy, be clear about this from the beginning. Aside from exceptional circumstances I do not recommend extending the number of sessions with such contracts. Also ask yourself if the number of sessions available is appropriate for the presenting issues. In long-term therapy I recommend a review after a few sessions before establishing an open-ended agreement.

Explain something about the process of gestalt therapy – Give a simple and concise account of the way you work. Be careful not to get too technical, there are enough invitations to do so with some of the gestalt terminology.

---

[23] United Kingdom Council for Psychotherapy.
[24] British Association of Counselling and Psychotherapy.

There is a certain paradox in the fact that we need firm and clear boundaries in place in relation to the therapeutic space to facilitate the possibility of healthy fluidity and permeability between client and therapist and their respective contact boundaries. The process of gestalt therapy with our dialogic focus on inclusion, presence and confirmation together with a desire for understanding how the client meets and makes sense of their world can lead to intimate relating between therapist and client.

At the end of the day a governing body or I can write about the importance of the maintenance of therapeutic boundaries and we can all nod in agreement. In the therapeutic relationship the most important field condition of all is not our ability to adhere to the rulebook, it is our attitude, our honest care for the wellbeing of our clients and our profession. We might make mistakes but in our bones we know right from wrong – what is more, I believe that our clients know that we do too.

89

Assessing risk

Implicit in therapy is stepping out and risking something unfamiliar, some novel way of being. Never ignore the risks that come with such a move. We need to assess risk at initial assessment with clients but as with all assessment this process will be on-going.

Even with the most depressed client, seeking therapy suggests some belief that the quality of their life can improve. Even if this ray of hope flickers dimly, it has shone brightly enough to get them to the therapy room. Concurrently, or shifting from their ground to figure, may be the desire or thoughts of committing the ultimate retroflection – suicide. If this is in the field I make a point of discussing what can be one of our cultural taboos openly with the client and differentiate between suicidal intent and suicidal ideation. There is a world of difference between thinking about an action and carrying this action out. As retroflection is marked by turning back an impulse and a hardening of the contact boundary, the very process of facilitating expression of suicidal thoughts and feelings can soften the contact boundary and reduce a sense of isolation. I believe this can reduce the chance of ideation being acted upon.

If risk to self or others is in the field, the 'here and now' can only offer a certain amount of information. There is considerable research suggesting that past behaviours in relation to self/other harm and suicide attempts are indicators of current risk. Bear in mind that risk to self or others does not just relate to suicide or violence but can include a wide range of behaviours: substance abuse, neglect of self and/or others, eating disorders, cutting oneself, addictive behaviours, compulsive risk taking, remaining in a grossly abusive relationship to name a few possible areas. To practise responsibly, ethically and in the interests of our client and their immediate field we need to take a history to gain as full a description as possible of the phenomenology of the behaviour. In doing so we need to strike a balance between curiosity and structure. Some areas I might explore are: When did the behaviour begin? Was there a specific trigger? What is the function of the behaviour? Does anyone else know? Has the intensity of this behaviour varied over time? What has supported this behaviour? This is by no means an exhaustive list and I suggest that any such assessment is weaved into the dialogue rather than run through as a checklist. You will probably naturally use this information in tandem with that gathered in relation to the client's use of contact functions (see Point 34).

Experiential exercise
Suicide, self-harm, sexual deviance – Consider your views in relation to these areas. How comfortable/uncomfortable would you feel about gaining a description from your client about these behaviours?

Some clients have a particularly erratic style of relating and can easily fragment when faced with stress. When clients with such relational patterns get angry they often retroflect their anger, harm themselves or even attempt suicide. Such clients require firm therapeutic boundaries and an experienced therapist when they are *borderlining*.

There are differing thoughts on managing clients who experience urges to commit suicide. Personally I ask for a commitment from the client that as long as they are in therapy with me they will not attempt suicide and make myself available for contact if they experience such impulses. When I am not available in person I provide telephone contact and/or contact with a locum therapist.

We also need to consider *therapeutic risk* when working with clients. Therapy can help bring about dramatic life changes and even though these may be positive, journeying through them can be stressful. 'What is ordinarily called "security" is clinging to the unfelt, declining the risk of the unknown involved in any absorbing satisfaction ... It is a dread of aggression, destroying and loss ... A better meaning for "security" would be the confidence of a firm support which comes from previous experience having been assimilated and growth achieved.' (PHG, 1951). In therapy clients need to journey through a phase of aggression and destroying old ways of being, old 'securities' have served them well in the past and now it may feel that there is nothing as the client faces the void. Such a process takes a certain amount of ego strength. If the client is insufficiently supported and led into solvent-based experimentation when glue is needed, fragmentation can occur.

In my final few words in this brief visit to the vast subject of risk assessment I would like to focus not on the client but on the therapist. What are the risks to you of working with such demands as those described above? What supports do you need, both inside and outside the therapy world? If you ask yourself such questions you will probably be more sensitive to your client's needs and model a healthy way of being – we are each part of the other's phenomenal field. When we meet with the other we learn about ourselves.

90

Attending to the wider field

A butterfly flaps its wings in Tibet and causes a tornado in Texas. This notion from chaos theory is not restricted to the world of meteorology. A small psychological shift can create the equivalent of a tornado of change in the client's field. Similarly situational change can stimulate enduring psychological change as the client's world-view is irrevocably altered. An obvious example might be the collapse of something that the client perceives as permanent or certain whether close to home or further afield – a marriage breakdown or a terrorist attack such as 9/11.

Experiential exercise
Think of a time when a more distant event might have altered your view of the world in some way. If you cannot think of such an example consider whether you believe that this is possible for you.

Although the therapy session takes place in a private, confidential setting it is not detached from the wider field. Something we need to be mindful of when working with clients is that they come to their therapy session from a wider situation and usually return to a similar situation. If that situation contains elements of risk, some of the creative adjustments that in the different context of the therapy room we might consider to be unhealthy 'interruptions' to contact, in that wider situation may maintain their safety. Behaviour always needs to be viewed in the context of where it manifests.

Parlett, in discussing the *unified field*, outlines, 'the web of interconnection between person and situation, self and others, organism and environment, the individual and the communal' (1997: 16). The relevance of field theory can be difficult to grasp, as this 'web of interconnection' can appear to include anything and everything. That butterfly in Tibet might as a consequence of flapping its wings affect things in the immediate field just as historical events will but there are layers of influence in a person's field. Whilst field events are connected they are also structured and organized with the figural issue at the centre. When a client comes to therapy many of the background field conditions will be out of awareness.

Let us consider a possible example of the impact of the wider field upon the immediate field. A client arrives for therapy suffering from anxiety. His description of his experience is one of feeling fearful, shattered, fragmented, 'in pieces'. This might be experienced as completely self-contained (within the client's own skin) or in relation to a narrow area of his field, for instance, a work-related problem and fear of redundancy. If we consider this presenting issue as solely the client's problem we journey down the road of anxiety management and an individualized treatment plan (which could be helpful in the short term). However, if we pan outwards from the immediate presentation and consider this experience of feeling shattered, fragmented and 'in pieces' to be a symptom of the person's field rather than of the individual, what might we see from that perspective? We may see a fragmenting industry in which the client has spent his working life, elements of his family past or present may be 'in pieces', and his children's schooling may be fragmenting. Pan out further and he may perceive an uncertain economy, a movement away from the communal and towards an isolated way of being fuelled by technological advances. The client walks around a planet many of whose inhabitants show a lack of care for their environment or are exploitative of its resources, resulting in the physical world coming under threat of its very existence. The sickness is not within the client; it is in the client's situation.

In discussing field theory Smuts saw a possible revolutionary reform in the way we conceptualize, 'for people to accustom themselves to the idea of fields, and to look upon every concrete thing or person or even abstract idea as merely a centre, surrounded by zones or auras or spheres of the same nature as the centre, only more attenuated and shading off into indefiniteness' (1926: 18–19). We may spend most of our time with our clients attending to the more central 'zones, auras or spheres' of the client's field. They are likely to present with a few central themes, but we must not lose sight of the influencing factors in the field that exist beyond the immediate.

According to Lewin (1952) behaviour is a function of the

current field conditions and the person and the environment are co-dependent with change in either affecting the whole. Any search for understanding begins with appreciation of the whole and follows with examining the component parts, not vice versa. It is worth repeating that the whole is more than the sum of the component parts. Discoveries in quantum physics revealing that nothing is fixed and that there are only constantly moving, inter-related fields of energy dancing their patterns throughout creation support the notion of a field-theoretical world.

91

Working with difference

As already stated in gestalt therapy we see each person's lifespace and the way in which they relate to their world as unique, so if we are all different let me clarify what is meant here by the term 'difference'. I am referring to difference here as being a member of a minority group which is disadvantaged because of difference.

Differences in given power and privilege are not always visible and when some areas are, such as a black woman being seen by a white male therapist, there are other elements on the outer levels of the laminated field that are less visible or invisible. The therapist's heritage, including a colonial past, or the black woman's ancestors having been slaves or servants for privileged whites are all part of the situation and will impact the situation. We could make similar comparisons with other areas such as disability, mental health problems, race, sexuality and any other area where the person is disadvantaged just by virtue of who they are.

With an eye on the laminated field and how this can preconfigure the relationship in the here and now let use consider our use of language in relation to difference:

Experiential exercise
Consider the following areas in tandem: Black person/White person, Gay man/Gay woman, Promiscuous man/Promiscuous woman, Male genitalia/Female genitalia. Write each down as headings on separate pieces of paper and brainstorm slang and colloquial terms that you are aware of for each. Think of as many as you can and be aware of any terms in the field that you are holding back from using. Take 15 to 20 minutes and then stand back and consider what these terms might say about these differences. You could repeat the exercise for other areas of difference if you wish, e.g. disability, mental health problems, learning difficulties.

Working with difference is a matter of conveying a healthy open attitude through dialogue, holding a genuine interest in the client's phenomenology in relation to their different way of perceiving, within a relationship that takes place in a field of current and historical influences. As therapists we also need to acknowledge our own ignorance and be prepared to redress this whilst being open to the idea that the way in which we use diagnosis can pathologize difference.[25] Although we will always learn from our clients, we could abuse our power if we hold some unaware expectation that they will educate us regarding their difference. Taking responsibility for broadening our knowledge of different cultures and difference will help to equalize the therapeutic relationship.

With our grounding in field theory, holism, phenomenology and dialogue together with our belief that self emerges in relation to other (difference), gestalt should be well placed for working with difference. However, like many other therapies there are huge areas where a disproportionately low number of minority groups have contact with our predominantly white, middle-class profession and its theories, predominantly constructed by white middle-class men. I do not believe that this will change without active moves out into the communities we wish to impact – the mountain is not going to come to Mohammad. In considering how we include we also need to consider how we exclude.

McConville (1997) discussed with openness his experience of bewilderment when working with adolescents of different skin colour. He realized that his well-intended actions could still be hurtful for the other. He conceptualized a process of the figure carrying the weight of the ground. If we think of what can be in the ground of a person with a different skin colour seeking therapy from a white person in terms of power, privilege and the historical field, that is one heavy figure! A similar dynamic is likely to play out in other relationships where there is a fundamental difference between therapist and client where the therapist is holding the privileged position. The therapist already holds a position of power and anything that tilts the balance further in their direction, whether figural or embedded in the relational

---

[25] It was not until 1973 that homosexuality was removed from the American Psychiatric Association's Diagnostic Manual.

ground, runs the risk of creating a relational fissure. It also offers the opportunity for a bridge with healing potential to be built across that difference.

I recall with embarrassment some of my clumsy early work with an African Caribbean man in the British National Health Service. In my enthusiasm to compensate for what I perceived as this man being misunderstood by the service, I omitted the basic steps of phenomenological inquiry and succeeded in defining his reality and missing him completely. I tried to align myself prematurely with this client being fearful that an expression of difference would jeopardize connection and inclusion. It was my client who clearly outlined our difference and provided me with a valuable lesson – that although difference can distance, the novel is required for contact and what is *is*.

As a white, British, professional, middle-class male, I occupy a privileged position in the UK. I also have a disability, am from a very working-class background and spent my educational years and early working life recovering from brain damage that handicapped my intellectual ability for many years. I might have experience of being in a prejudiced minority but my difference does not lay on the surface in the way that different skin colour, some disabilities and deformities do. Some differences can be hidden and others cannot and disclosure when one is in a minority lays one bare to the world of judgements. Disclosure of one's difference is not always a choice.

92

Sexual issues

I was participating in a workshop on sexual attraction and the erotic in therapy at an international residential training with a group of experienced gestalt therapists. We were asked to walk around the room and make eye contact with the mix of men and women whilst identifying to ourselves to whom we felt sexually attracted (different or same gender). One might have expected the breathing in the room to become heavier at that point but there was a collective holding of breath. This was followed by a collective sigh of relief (my meaning of the sigh might be my projection) when the facilitator announced that the next step in the exercise was not to reveal whom we had identified. One of my American colleagues exclaimed, 'Well thank goodness for that!' I think she was speaking for others as well as herself in that moment. I'd like to reiterate that these were a group of experienced gestalt therapists, and were representative of a spread of nationalities across the white western world. The powerful taboos about talking openly and directly about sexual attraction in many cultures were present in the repressed energy that escaped through laughter at the conclusion of that exercise.

Consider the following questions
If you were assessing a client for therapy would you ask them about their sex life? If so, what would you ask? If not, why not? Would you ask them about masturbation? Would this differ according to gender and sexual orientation?

The erotic has energy like nothing else. Yet when it is figural in the field between client and therapist, it is often deflected, retroflected or repressed. If it is discussed the 'safe option' of *aboutism* can often be adopted. Perhaps not without good reason we have moved to a position of caution for fear of the possible consequences of traumatizing our clients or a therapeutic intervention being misunderstood with the possible after-effects of accusations of professional malpractice. The societal field is intolerant of any error. In erring on the side of caution we avoid the obvious risks but we also avoid engaging with what can be a life-enhancing energy. The few therapists who have crossed the line between professional exploration and personal gratification have a lot to answer for.

O'Shea (2003) notes that, historically, erotic transference has been viewed pejoratively, being seen primarily through a critical lens of being a resistance to the therapy by the client. For the therapist erotic counter-transference has carried with it the damning and shameful judgement of immaturity (ibid). Both need to be viewed in the same light as any other transferential process – as information. Furthermore, as reality is co-created it follows that any sexual attraction that arises is co-created, therefore to be true to our gestalt principles we need to be thinking of and describing these dynamics as *erotic co-transference* since 'meaning is co-created by both subjectivities' (Sapriel, 1998: 42). One of the potential problems identified when viewing relational dynamics through a lens of counter-transference is that the therapist can use it as a sophisticated deflection from taking responsibility for their own responses (O'Shea, 2000; Mackewn, 1997).

As discussed the therapist/client relationship holds an imbalance of power, and power can be seductive. Re-stating the boundaries of the therapeutic relationship and ethical codes is safe practice but does not deal with the reality of any sexual attraction. It can help create an environment in which sexual attraction can be explored, but conversely if the dialogue is not handled carefully can induce a shame reaction in the client who might feel wrong for feeling a perfectly natural human reaction. There are plenty of unhealthy introjects we can inadvertently reinforce around sex, being sexual and the erotic. To further complicate an already complex field we have the contamination of terms such as 'erotic' through pornography.

I believe that one of the greatest challenges for any therapist is finding a way for sexual energy to be expressed safely within the therapeutic relationship. Sadly, due to responsible considerations for our clients and our own safety, it may not always be possible to do so with the openness with which we explore other areas. My experience from my training at two different gestalt training institutes here in the UK tallies with the experience of O'Shea (2003) on the other side of the globe, in that the subject of managing the dilemma of erotic transference was essentially sidestepped. It needs not to be.

93

Touch in therapy

Use of touch can be evocative, expressive and intimate. The word 'touch' is often used in language to indicate a deep-felt sense, as in 'I feel touched'. The degree to which we use touch in our relationships in Western culture generally indicates the degree of closeness in those relationships. Different types and qualities of touch are associated with sexual intimacy, friendships and business to name but three relational areas on a 'touch continuum' – as therapists we are in the business of intimate relating!

It is not surprising that the use of touch in therapy is controversial. The less tactile the culture, the more controversial it becomes – controversy fuelled by touch often being sexualized. Such cultural field conditions mean that we need to exercise caution in the use of touch in therapy. What is crucial is that the therapist pays due attention to their proactive material and I strongly recommend that use of touch is discussed in supervision before being practised. Out-of-awareness expression of sexual feelings, infantilizing, soothing emotions the therapist finds uncomfortable, creating/maintaining a hierarchy in the relationship can all be conveyed through the use of touch. The different dynamics of different gender and sexuality combinations between client and therapist further complicates this potential minefield.

As well as exercising discretion when using touch in therapy, we also need informed consent. It is useful for the therapist to give some explanation about how touch might possibly assist the client and, if it feels appropriate, a basic and understandable outline of your thinking. If the therapist is using touch in a specialized way they need to ensure that they have adequate training and supervision in using such techniques (Joyce and Sills, 2001). Let us also be mindful that we are practising an embodied therapy; if we touch 'the body' and not the person we objectify the client (Kepner, 1987).

Experiential exercise
Look around the room and choose an object. Study this object but do not touch it. Use your other senses to explore it thoroughly. Imagine what its texture may be, its weight, its solidity. Once you have done this thoroughly, for at least five minutes, explore the same object using touch. Note what new information you gather about the object and how the object strikes you, e.g. surprise at its coldness, comforted by its solidity.

When we touch we discover something about self, other and our relation to other that we could not have discovered otherwise. No matter how adept we are at describing or how acutely we attune our other senses, omit one realm of experience and there will be a realm of not knowing. Whilst there are sound ethical, therapeutic and protective (self and other) reasons for not employing the use of touch in therapy, a danger is that we then move away from an embodied way of relating to a more cognitive form of relating. Conversely, Paul Barber in a moving account of his experience of his therapy with the late Miriam Polster says, 'She never touched me yet I felt caressed and held' (2002a: 76). I have heard similar experiences of feeling held without the need for actual touch. Perhaps we should not underestimate our capacity to hold clients with our eyes, with our compassion and our way of being. We can work with the client's body and in an embodied way without using touch by: noticing body movements and posture, using embodied language, introducing movement, inviting body-oriented experiments, using tactile experimentation such as sand tray.

I would always advocate erring on the side of caution when using touch, quite simply: if in any doubt don't touch. Whether we use touch or not, it is useful to consider whether you would or wouldn't like physical contact with your client and what meaning this may have for this relationship. I am saddened by the inevitable limiting field conditions surrounding the use of touch in therapy. Developmentally it is one of the first ways we got to know our world, before sight, before description. Kepner (2001) offers us a sobering thought with his observation that infants who lack touch die and those that receive sufficient physical contact thrive; it is the predominant mode of communication for the infant. Careful use of touch can offer powerful healing and however valid the ethical arguments against employing touch in therapy, no ethical code will ever remove the longing for the touch-deprived client. Perhaps it must be out in their world rather than in the therapy room that clients need to satisfy such a need.

94

Gestalt supervision

In the UK it is a requirement for therapists to be in regular supervision for as long as they are working as counsellors or psychotherapists. So what is supervision? The colloquial use of the terms supervision and supervisor can lead to some misconceptions. The uninitiated can gain the impression that supervision is simply telling the therapist what to do as a supervisor in industry might. Whilst some guidance is often needed to ensure safe practice, particularly for those new to the profession, this needs to be balanced with allowing the supervisee space to develop their own philosophy as a therapist. The function of gestalt supervision is not to provide the supervisee with an armoury of techniques and interventions, but to assist them in understanding the co-created dynamics of the therapeutic relationship.

The process of supervision has been described as being a form of meta-therapy (Hess, 1980; Hawkins and Shohet, 1989/2000; Gilbert & Evans, 2000), meaning that what is evoked between supervisor and supervisee often parallels characteristics of the client/therapist relationship. These parallel processes can be seen as conceptual bridges between therapy and supervision. A range of resistances can be paralleled that block movement; supervisee and supervisor can play out varying shades of the dynamics present in the client/therapist relationship and naming such processes is often useful.

Modelling a healthy process in the supervisory relationship provides powerful experiential learning. At the beginning of the supervisory relationship it is important to complete groundwork tasks in much the same way that we outline therapeutic boundaries (see Point 88). Another parallel is that the supervisor needs to strike a balance between adequately addressing these areas and not flooding the new supervisee with information. This is an opportunity for the supervisor to model a process-focused way of delivering such information. Structure is needed to facilitate freedom and creativity in supervision just as it is in therapy.

On the subject of structure I offer the following focusing menu for supervision adapted from the works of Hawkins and Shohet (2000) and Gilbert and Clarkson (1991).

1. Exploration of therapeutic strategies and interventions with a focus on expanding the therapist's range and variation, whilst acknowledging what they do well.
2. Process-focused exploration of the therapeutic relationship. What patterns are emerging in the relationship?
3. Exploration of transference phenomena including a focus on the relationship of the here-and-now of the therapy session to other space/time zones. For example, what might be paralleling here from other relationships?
4. A diagnostic focus. This might be describing diagnosis in relation to gestalt maps, character styles or discussing psychiatric diagnostic terms through a gestalt lens.
5. The application of theory to practice and practice to theory – the latter could include identifying unconscious competence.
6. Relating what is happening in the therapy room to the wider field.
7. Moral and ethical dilemmas.
8. Celebration and review of what the therapist has done well.

The supervision session is likely to move between different areas as the presenting focus recedes into the ground and a different supervisory need becomes figural. Parallel processes can again provide a possible window into the client's way of relating, e.g. a supervisee discussing a deflecting client who is avoiding addressing an issue may dance around a host of the above foci and avoid addressing any of them.

- Just as gestalt therapy uses phenomenological focusing and experimentation to clarify the experience of the client so gestalt supervision uses phenomenological methods to clarify the experience of the supervisee in relation to their client (Yontef, 1996).
- Just as gestalt therapy has a field focus viewing the situation as being in a constant state of flux, so gestalt supervision

relates to the whole lifespace, valuing no single aspect as potentially more relevant than any other.

• Just as gestalt therapy engages in dialogue within a horizontal relationship, so gestalt supervision seeks to understand at an embodied level the client's experience through the supervisee through dialogue.

As the supervisor's focus is primarily on the therapeutic relationship many interactions with the supervisee will be I-It rather than I-Thou. The supervisor therefore needs to hold an I-Thou attitude with the supervisee, acknowledging the preconfiguring dynamics of the relationship.

With reference to Nevis (1987) I would like to draw the following analogy with the process of gestalt supervision. Developing a synthesis of feeling and thinking can be likened to playing the piano. The left hand keeps the beat and that is what the supervisor does, teaches people how to get a sense of rhythm and timing. The right hand is the melody, the more expressive part where you are more authentically present. To practise competently, with structure, and to communicate with other pianists (therapists), an ability to read and write music is needed (learn the theory of psychotherapy). To do all of this together well requires practice and dedication.

95

Therapist support

We work intimately with many of our clients but those relationships are rightly boundaried and limited. There are some clients I could happily have had as friends had we met under different circumstances. However, once we have worked as someone's therapist we always need to view the relationship through that pre-configuring lens with all its restrictions. Ethical guidelines support this view. Although there are some variations that suggest a transition from a therapeutic relationship to a social relationship is possible after a certain period of time, I do not subscribe to this view. One of the paradoxes in our work is that in a relationship-focused profession we can simultaneously find ourselves living an isolated existence. In preserving confidentiality I am not able to chat about my work with my wife over dinner in the same way that she is about her day teaching music. From gestalt's field perspective if we are insufficiently supported as therapists this will be communicated to our clients. This is one of the reasons I say allow yourself to be passionate about working as a therapist, but do not make therapy your only passion.

In what can be demanding work with clients who might feel that they are disintegrating in worlds that they experience as falling apart, the therapist needs to be standing on firm and supporting ground. As we are repeatedly exposed to traumatic experiences we are vulnerable to vicarious traumatization. Professional supports such as supervision, peer supervision, conferences and continued professional development are of course important, but to feed the therapist, build wider support and counter the possibility of burnout, so is smelling the coffee in the therapist's wider field. There is a possible danger of isolation or even alienation from the therapist's wider lifespace if one immerses oneself totally in the field of therapy. If we look at this potential from a systems perspective and take it to an extreme, it is possible for the world of therapy to alienate itself from whole sections of the society it hopes to serve. Our clients can serve as mirrors for our own potential to isolate ourselves individually and collectively. A sobering thought is offered by Farber (1966) who comments on the effects of alienation in relation to I-It and I-Thou relating in noting that the more alienated one is, the less one can rejoice in either I-It or I-Thou relating. Although this observation is made discussing clients, it is equally applicable to therapists and seems to me to equate with the possibility of therapist burnout.

Gestalt therapy training can inadvertently model a process of intense immersion into the field of gestalt therapy theory and practice to the exclusion of all other diversions, and I do not presume this is peculiar to gestalt. The next training task becomes immediately figural before satisfaction over the last training task has had an opportunity to emerge. The post-contact phase of the cycle is denied space. Whilst training is often stimulating and exciting, let us not lose sight of our need for withdrawal and leaving space for the possibility of a fertile void emerging – where fresh creativity may be born. Let us live the change we want to see in the worlds of our clients.

Part 6

RESEARCH AND EVALUATING THE APPROACH: DESTINATION AND LOOKING BACK

96

Gestalt's spiritual traditions and the transpersonal

The terms 'transpersonal' and 'spiritual' are often used inter-changeably. The roots of gestalt therapy's spiritual tradition and its Eastern influences are evident in its founders' various studies in spiritual philosophy. Laura Perls studied with the existential philosopher Martin Buber whilst Fritz Perls studied Zen Buddhism and existential philosophy. Both Laura Perls and Paul Goodman followed their considerable interest in Taoism. The title given to a collection of Goodman's essays, *Nature Heals* (1977), stems from his Taoist principles of living with nature in accordance with the ways of nature. This fits with the later development and integration of the Paradoxical Theory of Change (Beisser, 1970) into gestalt. Many of the here-and-now focused awareness exercises in PHG (1951) have a flavour of being influenced by Zen meditations. The Zen Buddhist, Crook, sees a 'fundamental convergence between Buddhist thought and the developing theory underlying Gestalt therapy' (2001: 40), the two sharing a similar belief in 'the field.' Although Zen got there before gestalt by some 2,500 years, their eventual convergence is evident in gestalt field theory's belief in an inter-relating reality. Both philosophies promote an acceptance of *what is* without aiming for change.

With regard to Zen and gestalt's focus on immediate here-and-now experience, I recall a client telling me of an exercise he had completed on a residential course. He explained that he paired up with someone and was slowly and repeatedly asked, 'Who are you?' for a considerable period of time. This exercise took place on a Zen Buddhist retreat but from my client's description it could just as easily have taken place on a gestalt therapy workshop.

Both Taoist and Zen Buddhist traditions have influenced gestalt's belief in the need to stay with experience rather than forcibly 'move on'. The concept and belief in the value of the fertile void emerged from the founders' studies of Eastern philosophies and existentialism. Taoist belief that opposites exist throughout all of nature, encapsulated in the concept of yin and yang, is mirrored in gestalt's thinking around polarities (see Point 81), and the gestalt notion of *organismic self-regulation* is not a million miles from the Taoist doctrine of inaction.

I see personal connection to the other as a spiritual event, as in the I-Thou moment discussed by Buber (see Point 63) when boundaries dissolve in moments of intimate knowing. Just as an I-Thou moment cannot be forced but emerges through grace, I cannot *have* spirituality, it emerges between the other and me, whether that *other* is a person, a landscape, a piece of art or a god. It is a human being's deepest form of connection and experiencing the I-Thou moment transforms I-It relating in a similar way to how a spiritual experience transforms ordinary experience. The following displays something of the spirituality inherent in the integration of Buber's work into gestalt, co-creation and gestalt's belief in self as process: 'far from becoming an organism that takes in what it wants from the environment, we become a self only through meeting other selves in an I-Thou relationship' (Friedman, 1990). Spirituality and spiritual tradition can provide a sense of connectedness and a moral code within an individualistic culture.

As we might expect there are many different and varied views on spirituality[26] within gestalt. Kennedy describes the gestalt approach not merely as a form of therapy but as a way of being in the world and a way of understanding ourselves that is 'congenial to a personal spirituality' (1998: 88). Somewhere towards the opposite end of the spectrum is the view that promotion of spirituality within gestalt is both unnecessary and undeserving of major consideration in gestalt therapy (Feder, 2001). As with other aspects of gestalt therapy it lies with the individual therapist to develop their own philosophy in relation to spirituality, the transpersonal and gestalt. Just like our clients we need to find a place to stand in relation to our spiritual beliefs and how we integrate these into our approach, and that place may change.

---

[26] For a more extensive overview on spirituality, the transpersonal and gestalt, I would like to direct the interested reader to Lynn Williams' (2006) well-researched paper.

97

Research and appropriate research paradigms

As gestalt therapists we are natural researchers, our approach is geared towards uncovering the way in which we relate to the world, what we experience, how we form experience. We research acts of intentionality, field conditions including the cultural ground through exploration of the client's lifespace and ways of limiting and expanding awareness. We are in the business of holistic research.

Qualitative and quantitative researches are two very different animals in the research world. In the table below I have listed a few of the basic differences in the methodology, aims and beliefs of each.

Table 6.1 shows that the methodology in qualitative research is far more like 'home territory' to gestalt therapists than a quantitative research paradigm. The two different research methodologies can be set up as being in opposition but they do not need to be viewed as polar opposites. Elements of each can be integrated in mixed-method research (also called pluralistic research). I see the development and integration of aspects of quantitative research methods as a growing edge in gestalt therapy together with a wider sharing of the qualitative research that has been carried out. As a therapy that specializes in integration and the resolution of conflict through creative adjustment, gestalt should be well placed to achieve such a task. When conducting research we need to be consistent with the practice of gestalt therapy bearing in mind that 'a great researcher does not shun the painful contradictory evidence to his theory but seeks it out to enlarge and deepen the theory' (PHG, 1951: 249).

Basing his approach on the gestalt approach to inquiry, Barber (2006) argues passionately against the pursuit of a single truth – such a reductionist stance would be antithetical to gestalt – by what he refers to as the researcher practitioner. Barber sees the researcher as uncovering 'the portrayal of truth as a whole . . . where the researcher *is the research* in contrast to merely doing or

Table 6.1

Quantitative research	Qualitative research
Involves a large number of respondents.	Sample size is less important and is smaller, emphasis on the richness of the sample.
Questions are structured.	Questions are open and seek description.
Considered objective and is concerned with statistics.	Collects subjective data.
Concerned more with numbers, counting and measuring.	Concerned with meanings, concepts, description and characteristics.
Tests theory.	Develops theory.
Is measureable.	Is interpretive.
Conducted in a controlled outcome-orientd setting.	Conducted in a more natural setting and is process oriented.
Seeks generalizations in order to predict, leading to understanding and explanation.	Seeks difference and the development of patterns for understanding.
Data is not collected until all aspects of the study are designed.	Design emerges as the study unfolds.
Researcher remains at an objective distance.	Researcher becomes subjectively immersed.
'Hard' science.	'Soft' science.

being it' (2002b: 79). He goes on to describe qualitative methods that are allied to gestalt, a heavily edited selection of which I have listed below:[27]

• *Naturalistic Inquiry* – Research is carried out in the subject's natural setting. It is a research-based phenomenological inquiry where meaning emerges between the researcher and the researched.

---

[27] With thanks to Paul Barber for his kind permission and apologies for the holes this précis of his fine work leaves. For the interested researcher I suggest studying Barber's 2006 publication.

- *Ethnography* – A form of research that focuses on a group's culture or community through close field observation of socio-cultural phenomena. 'Ethnography looks for the ways culture, tradition and idiosyncratic meaning shape individual and collective behaviour' (Barber, 2006: 70).
- *Action Research* – The term is credited to Kurt Lewin, the founder of gestalt field theory. The process spirals through four phases in a cycle, these phases being: planning, acting, observing/evaluating, reflecting (and then back to planning).
- *Field Theory* – Studying the total situation.
- *Grounded Theory* – The theory is developed from the data collected making this an inductive approach in that it moves from the specific to the wider field.
- *Holistic Inquiry* – This approach to research embraces the notion that the whole is greater than the sum of its parts and the interdependence of those parts. If we study the parts separately they change, i.e. exploring behaviour out of context.
- *Heuristic Research* – Requires a personal connection with the research topic, aiming to explore the essence of the person in the experience and as such 'autobiographical, and meditative reflections come especially to the fore' (ibid).

98

Applications of gestalt beyond 1:1 and group therapy

Possible applications of gestalt therapy beyond what we may consider to be 'the clinical setting' are wide ranging. If we embrace gestalt's field perspective we need to pay greater attention to what interventions could be made to improve others' situations. In the West we tend to deal with problem areas by splitting them off from the rest of society rather than seeing them as a part of our society. The so-called 'mentally ill' are actually or metaphorically institutionalized, as are the old and infirm, whilst offenders are locked away. With greater inclusion and the problem being viewed as a societal problem rather than an individual problem, more of these people could move to fit into a more accommodating society. Our society could also allow itself the opportunity of addressing an underlying societal condition that manifests in such symptoms. This may appear radical, simplistic and unrealistically idealistic but there will be small steps that we can make towards greater integration and inclusion. As we have seen, gestalt deals with wholes and implicit in its field approach is a systems perspective and co-creation.

Gestalt is as much a philosophy as it is a therapy and as such a gestalt philosophy can be applied to a variety of settings to help facilitate healthy functioning. It is already well established in working with small systems such as couples and families and there are successful and well-established courses teaching the application of gestalt in organizations and organizational consulting here in the UK and overseas.[28]

Since gestalt moved on from a 'figure-bound' way of working in its early days (Wheeler, 1991), it is the gestalt approach's ability to explore the structure of the ground from which organization of

---

[28] Two such established training institutes running such courses are Metanoia in the UK and The Cleveland Institute in the USA.

the figure emerges that lends gestalt to a wide range of applications way beyond individual and group therapy. In its application the figural problem is explored in relation to the ground from which it emerged rather than the figural problem being examined in isolation. For example a question such as, 'Why is this child underperforming in this school?' would be re-framed to have a more phenomenological and field focus such as, 'what is reflected in this child's behaviour that mirrors patterns of relating in the school? What is the child representing for the whole system? We could just as easily substitute 'child' and 'school' with 'employee' and 'office', 'department' and 'company', 'ward' and 'hospital' or any example of a smaller system within a larger system.

Chidiac and Denham-Vaughan discuss the application of the concept of id, ego and personality functions and gestalt's notion of self as process in their work with organizations. Whilst acknowledging what presents on the surface and is known (ego function) is important, they focus on the id functioning as they believe this holds greater potential for change if awareness can be raised of 'what lurks underneath' (2009: 47). This tallies with the belief in gestalt that change occurs in the ground.

One of gestalt therapy's elder statesmen, Philip Lichtenberg, lives in a retirement community where although the population of 350 are not gestalt therapists, the community does practise gestalt principles. He teaches courses within this community, and its members are still active in the wider community whilst receiving the support they require when they require it. Compare this with some of the one-size-fits-all retirement homes in the UK and elsewhere and the way the elderly are implicitly devalued. Lichtenberg (2007) talks about the need for gestalt therapists to reach out to change everyday life in daily conversation, to engage in dialogue.

Being a gestalt therapist is not a coat we put on and take off – we need to live our lives by embracing the principles of our profession. We need to be active politically, organizationally, in our everyday life, ecologically as well as with our clients. In doing so we will impact those around us and move towards living more harmoniously in relation to others and our planet. The wider applications of gestalt are wide indeed.

99

Looking back and reviewing

In a healthy learning process we look back over material covered, chew it over and consider what aspects we agree with and what we disagree with – we quite literally 're-view'. Alternatively, we introject the material perhaps for consideration and assimilation later. As discussed earlier (see Point 86) reviewing is part of the ending phase of a therapy relationship where the emphasis is rightly placed on the client's experience, but learning in any relationship is a two-way process. I learn something from every client that I meet. It is important to set time aside to review your experience as a therapist to appreciate the work you have done, consider possible blind spots that may become more visible from a distance and reflect on possible areas of development. I advocate this review process at the end of therapy, but equally it could be a valuable exercise in self-supervision to conduct such a self-review during therapy. Such a process can focus the therapist by considering whether a variation in their approach or a change of therapeutic strategy is indicated. Here are some suggested questions that may help focus the therapist when reviewing and evaluating their therapeutic work:

What did I do well?
What do I regret?
Is there anything that I would like to remind myself about for work with other clients?
What sense do I make of our journey in relation to gestalt theory?
What will I remember most about this relationship?
What would I do differently if I had a re-wind button?
What is my growing edge as a therapist?

As you answer these questions note whether you tend to veer towards being negatively critical rather than constructively critical. If you do, then consider what might be positive in the 'mistakes' you made. Throughout this book I have emphasized our cultural pattern of moving rapidly onto the next task, avoiding satisfaction, withdrawal and time in the void – short-cutting the post-contact phase of the gestalt cycle. Through a process of review we can counter this cultural ground introject whilst simultaneously generating subjective research data for either formal or informal evaluation (see Point 97).

As we near the end of this book and this particular journey, I would like to invite you into a review of your learning experience in relation to the preceding points. Again I offer a few questions:

What have I found helpful?
What have I found unhelpful?
What have I found difficult to understand?
What do I tell myself when I have found something difficult to understand?
Are there any points that I would have liked to have seen covered that weren't?
Are there areas that I would like to study further?

I have constructed the above questions in the hope of helping to facilitate a movement from a simple awareness such as, 'I want to learn something about gestalt' to a more reflexive awareness in how you learn about gestalt, an awareness of your learning process and your patterns of becoming aware and blocking awareness, leading to 'awareness of one's overall awareness process' (Yontef, 1993: 251) in relation to learning. Looking back to the there and then can help facilitate greater awareness and increased contact in the here and now and offer possible direction for the future.

100

On uncertainty [29]

In gestalt therapy we need to tolerate the uncertainty of intersubjective relating, of not knowing what is going to come next. Such uncertainty can be joyful, fearful, exciting and anxiety-provoking but uncertainty is the only thing that makes life possible. Uncertainty is embedded in the roots of gestalt's phenomenological, field and existential philosophy. Over the course of this book I have discussed the unique ways in which we all view our worlds – different perceptions of different phenomenal worlds in a shared world. We all interpret, this is an existential given, but there is choice in the degree to which we remain tied to our certitudes. Gestalt therapists, just like anyone else, can stubbornly resist information that throws their world-view into question. A sound theoretical underpinning is essential for the gestalt therapist to practice competently and ethically, but we need to constantly review our theories in relation to the person or persons before us in our ever-changing field. A fixed and rigid theory is a way of creating an illusion of certainty in a world where the only certainty is change. It also restricts the growth of the client, the therapist and the profession. Without openness to change and revision, a preferred theory or concept can become a fit-all dogma, growth is stifled and the therapy exists rather than lives. The young child who views their world with an innocent fascination and freshness has a great deal to teach us therapists.

Some self-styled and poorly trained individuals do choose to practise a manualized form of so-called 'gestalt therapy' through stereotyped, rehearsed exercises and routine interventions, often with a fixed focus on 'anger work' and 'the empty chair'. Such unethical practice, which I am at pains to distance myself from, can create an illusion of certainty and pseudo-confidence but

---

[29] The title for this final point was inspired by Staemmler's 1997 paper 'Cultivating Uncertainty: An Attitude for Gestalt Therapists'.

its place belongs in the performing arts rather than the therapy room.

As in life, uncertainty permeates every aspect of gestalt therapy, illustrated in the integration of field theory in the approach. In the process of dialogue with our clients we need not to know the next step, for if we tell ourselves that we do we cement I-It relating.

Our belief in the non-existence of an isolated, fixed self but that self is fluid and forms in the process of relating means that we remain open to the unpredictable. Patterns of relating will form (most probably!), but within those patterns let us remain open to the twists and turns that break with any diagnostic picture of the client behaving 'narcissistically', 'depressively', 'anxiously' or when someone 'borderlines'. It is often those moments that most stimulate my interest, after all for something to change in our world we need to be doing something differently in our world.

'To cultivate uncertainty means to become *optimistic* and to expect change to be possible ... It also means to be ready to throw any impression of our clients out of the window again, if necessary right after you have had it, so that you are *open* to form new pictures again and again.'

(Staemmler, 1997: 47, original italics)

Human beings are complex and live and breathe in complex and intricate systems. The more complexity there, is the more uncertainty there is. The aim of gestalt is to increase awareness and increased awareness invariably leads to an expansion of the person's physical and psychological environment and with it a further increase in uncertainty. But let me conclude with one final thought as I glance over the top of my laptop to the cover of PHG, gestalt therapy's founding text. That uncertainty is a key ingredient in

'Excitement and Growth in Human Personality'.

(PHG, 1951: Front cover)

References

Barber, P. (2002a) 'Remembering Miriam Polster', *British Gestalt Journal* 11 (2): 76–79.

Barber, P. (2002b) 'Gestalt – A Prime Medium for Holistic Research and Whole Person Education', *British Gestalt Journal*, 11 (2): 78–90

Barber, P. (2006) *Becoming a Practitioner Researcher: A Gestalt Approach to Holistic Inquiry*. Middlesex University Press.

Beaumont, H. (1993) 'Martin Buber's "I-Thou" and Fragile Self Organization: Contributions to a Gestalt Couples Therapy', *British Gestalt Journal* 2 (2): 85–95.

Beisser, A. (1970) 'The Paradoxical Theory of Change', in Fagan, J. and Shepherd, I. (eds) *Gestalt Therapy Now*, New York: Harper.

Blake, W. (1977) *William Blake: The Complete Poems*. Alicia Ostricher (ed), London: Penguin Classics.

Bloom, D. (2003) 'Tiger! Tiger! Burning Bright', in Spagnuolo-Lobb, M. and Amendt-Lyon, N. (eds), *Creative Licence: The Art of Gestalt Therapy*. New York: Springer-Verlag.

Bloom, D. (2005) 'Revisiting the Aesthetic Criterion A Response to Sylvia Crocker', *British Gestalt Journal*, 14 (1): 54–56.

Bloom, D., Spagnuolo-Lobb, M. and Staemmler, F. (2008) 'Notes on Nomenclature', *Studies in Gestalt Therapy: Dialogical Bridges*, 2 (1).

Buber, M. (1958) *I and Thou*, 2nd Edition. Edinburgh: T & T Clark. (original published 1923).

Buber, M. (1965a) *The Knowledge of Man: A Philosophy of the Inter-human*. New York: Harper & Row.

Buber, M. (1965b) *Between Man and Man*. New York: MacMillan.

Buber, M. (1967) *A Believing Humanism: Gleanings*. New York: Simon & Schuster.

Buber, M. (1973) *Meetings*. LaSalle, IL: Open Court Publishing Co.

Chidiac, M-A. and Denham-Vaughan, S. (2007) 'The Process of Presence: Energetic Availability and Fluid Responsiveness', *British Gestalt Journal*, 16 (1): 9–19.

Chidiac, M-A. and Denham-Vaughan, S. (2009) 'An Organisational Self:

Applying the Concept of Self to Groups and Organisations', *British Gestalt Journal*, 18 (1): 42–49.

Clarkson, P. (1989) *Gestalt Counselling in Action*. London: Sage.

Crocker, S. (2004) 'Creativity in Gestalt Therapy: Book Review Essay', *British Gestalt Journal*, 13 (2): 126–134.

Crocker, S. (2005) 'Still Questioning the Aesthetic Criterion: A Reply to Bloom', *British Gestalt Journal*, 14 (1): 56–59.

Crook, J. (2001) 'Buddhism and Gestalt Therapy: A Response to Ruth Wolfert', *British Gestalt Journal*, 10 (1): 43–44.

cummings, e. e. (1994) In Firmage, G. (ed.) *Complete Poems 1904–1962*. New York: Liveright Publishing Corporation.

Delisle, G. (1999) *Balises II: A Gestalt Perspective on Personality Disorders*. Montreal: Le Reflet.

Denham-Vaughan, S. (2005) 'Will and Grace: An Integrative Dialectic Central to Gestalt Psychotherapy', *British Gestalt Journal*, 14 (1): 5–14.

Fagan, J. and Shepherd, I. (eds) (1971) *Gestalt Therapy Now: Theory, Techniques, Applications*. Palo Alto, CA: Science and Behavior Books.

Farber, L. (1966) *The Ways of the Will*. New York: Basic Books.

Feder, B. (2001) 'Spirituality: Irrelevant to Gestalt Therapy: A Response to Ruth Wolfert', *British Gestalt Journal*, 10 (1): 43–44.

Feder, B. (2006) *Gestalt Group Therapy: A Practical Guide*. New Orleans: Gestalt Institute Press.

Fodor, I. (1998) 'Awareness and Meaning Making: The Dance of Experience', *Gestalt Review*, 2 (1): 50–71.

Frank, R. (2001) *Body of Awareness: A Somatic and Developmental Approach to Psychotherapy*. Cambridge, Massachusetts: Gestalt Press.

Freud, S. (1997) The Interpretation of Dreams, Ware, Hertfordshire: Wordsworth Editions Ltd.

Friedlaender, S. (1918) *Schöpferische Indifferenz* (Creative indifference). München: Reinhardt.

Friedman, M. (1976) 'Healing through Meeting: A Dialogical Approach to Psychotherapy and Family Therapy, in Smith, J. (ed.) *Psychiatry and the Humanities*, 191–234. New Haven: Yate University Press.

Friedman, M. (1990) 'Dialogue, Philosophical Anthropology and Gestalt Therapy', *The Gestalt Journal*, XIII (1): 7–40.

From, I. and Muller, B. (1977) *Didactical notes* in Muller, B. (1996) 'Isadore From's Contributions to the Theory and Practice of Gestalt Therapy', *The Gestalt Journal* xix (1): 57–81.

Gilbert, M. and Clarkson, P. (1991) 'The Training of Counselling Trainers and Supervisors', in Dryden, W and Thorne, B (eds), *Training and Supervision for Counselling in Action*. London: Sage.

Gilbert, M. & Evans, K. (2000) *Psychotherapy Supervision: an integrative relational approach to psychotherapy supervision*. Buckingham: Open University Press.

Goethe, J. W. V. (1998) *Maxims and Reflections*. London: Penguin Books.

Goldstein, K. (1939) *The Organism*. New York: American Book.

Goodman, P. (1977) *Nature Heals: The Psychological Essays of Paul Goodman*. T. Stoehr (ed.), New York: Free Life Additions.

Greenberg, E. (1989) 'Healing the Borderline', *Gestalt Journal*, XII (2): 11–55.

Harris, J. (2007) 'Enjoying Groups: A Review of Gestalt Group Therapy: A Practical Guide', *British Gestalt Journal*, 16 (1): 59–62.

Hawkins, P. and Shohet, R. (2000) *Supervision in the Helping Professions*, 2nd edition. Buckingham: Open University Press.

Heidegger, M. (1962) *Being and Time*. Translated by J. Macquarrie and Robinson, E. New York: Harper & Row.

Hess, A. K. (ed.) (1980) *Psychotherapy Supervision: Theory, Research and Practice*. New York: Wiley.

Husserl, E. (1931) *Ideas: General Introduction to Pure Phenomenology*, Vol 1. New York: MacMillan.

Hycner, R. (1985) 'Dialogical Gestalt Therapy: An Initial Proposal', *The Gestalt Journal*, 8 (1): 23–49.

Hycner, R. (1989) 'The I-Thou Relationship and Gestalt Therapy: Based on panel discussion on Dialogical Gestalt, 11th Gestalt Conference', *The Gestalt Journal*, 1990. 13 (1): 41–54.

Hycner, R. (1993) *Between Person and Person: Toward a Dialogical Psychotherapy*. Highland, NY: Gestalt Journal Press.

Hycner, R. and Jacobs, L. (1995) *The Healing Relationship in Gestalt Therapy – A Dialogic / Self Psychology Approach*. Highland, NY: Gestalt Journal Press.

Idhe, D. (1977) *Experimental Phenomenology: An Introduction*. Albany: State University of New York.

Jacobs, L. (1992) 'Insights from Psychoanalytic Self-Psychology and Inter-Subjectivity Theory for Gestalt Therapists', *The Gestalt Journal*, XV (2): 25–61.

Jacobs, L. (1995) 'Shame in the Therapeutic Dialogue', *British Gestalt Journal*, 4 (2): 86–90.

Jacobs, L. (2000) 'For Whites Only', *British Gestalt Journal*, 9 (1): 3–14.

Jacobs, L. (2007) 'Self, Subject and Intersubjectivity', *Studies in Gestalt Therapy: Dialogical Bridges*, 1 (1).

Joyce, P. and Sills, C. (2001) *Skills in Gestalt Counselling & Psychotherapy*. London: Sage.

Kafka, F. (2005) *Investigations of a Dog in Franz Kafka: The Complete Short Stories*. London: Vintage.

Keating, F. (2007) *African and Caribbean Men and Mental Health*. London: Race Equality Foundation.

Kennedy, D. (1998) 'Gestalt: A Point of Departure for a Personal Spirituality', *British Gestalt Journal* 7 (2).

Kepner, E. (1980) 'Gestalt Group Process', in Feder, B. & Ronall, R. (eds), *Beyond the Hot Seat: Gestalt Approaches to Group*. New York: Brunner-Mazel.

Kepner, J. (1987) *Body Process: A Gestalt Approach to Working with the Body in Psychotherapy*. New York: Gardner.

Kepner, J. (2001) 'Touch in Gestalt Body Process Psychotherapy: Purpose, Practice, and Ethics', *Gestalt Review*, 5 (2): 97–114.

Kepner, J. (2003) 'The Embodied Field', *British Gestalt Journal*, 12 (1): 6–14.

Kitzler, R., Perls, L. and Stern, M. (1982) 'Retrospects and Prospects: A Trialogue between Laura Perls, Richard Kitzler and Mark Stern', *Voices*, 18 (2): 5–22.

Klein, M. (1946) 'Notes on some Schizoid Mechanisms', *The International Journal of Psychoanalysis*, 27 (3/4): 99–110.

Koffka, K. (1935) *Principles of Gestalt Psychology*. New York: Harcourt, Brace and World.

Korb, M (1999) 'Redefining Maturity and Maturational Processes'. *Gestalt Journal*, XXII (2): 7–30.

Latner, J. (1985) 'What Kinds of Figures does Gestalt Therapy Cut?' *Gestalt Journal*, VIII (1): 55–60.

Lee, R. (1995) 'Gestalt and Shame: The Foundations for a Clearer Understanding of Field Dynamics', *British Gestalt Journal* 4 (1): 14–22.

Lee, R. and Wheeler, G. (1996) (eds) *The Voice of Shame: Silence and Connection in Psychotherapy*. Cambridge, MA: Gestalt Press.

Levitsky A. and Perls F. (1970) 'The Rules and Games of Gestalt Therapy' in Fagan, J. and Shepherd, I. (eds.) *Gestalt Therapy Now*. Palo Alto: Harper.

Lewin, K. (1935) *A Dynamic Theory of Personality Selected Papers*. New York: McGraw-Hill.

Lewin, K. (1936) *Principles of Topological Psychology*. New York: McGraw-Hill.

Lewin, K. (1938) 'Will and Need', in W. Ellis (ed.), *A Source Book of Gestalt Psychology*. London: Routledge & Kegan Paul Ltd.

Lewin, K. (1952) *Field Theory in Social Sciences*. London: Tavistock.

Lichtenberg, P. (1991) 'Intimacy, Autonomy and Merging', *Gestalt Journal* XIV (1): 27–44.

Lichtenberg, P. (2007) 'Radical Relationships – interviewed by Christine Stevens', *British Gestalt Journal*, 16 (1): 28–34.

Lichtenberg, P. (2008) 'Culture Change: Conversations Concerning Political and Religious Difference', *Studies in in Gestalt Therapy: Dialogical Bridges*, 2 (1): 45–68.

MacKewn, J. (1997) *Developing Gestalt Counselling*. London: Sage.

McConville, M. (1997) 'The Gift', *Voice. Gestalt Institute of Cleveland*, 4: 11–15.

McConville, M. (2001) 'Lewinian Field Theory, Adolescent Development and Psychotherapy' in McConville, M. and Wheeler, G. (eds), *The Heart of Development: Gestalt approaches to Working with Children, Adolescents and their Worlds*: Vol 2. Hillsdale, NJ: Analytic Press.

McLeod, L. (1993) 'The Self in Gestalt Therapy Theory', *British Gestalt Journal*, 2 (1): 25–40.

Marrow, A. J. (1969) *The Practical Theorist: The Life and Work of Kurt Lewin*. New York: Basic Books.

Mazur, E. (1996) 'The Zeigarnik Effect and the Concept of Unfinished Business in Gestalt Therapy', *British Gestalt Journal*, 5 (1):18–23.

Melnick, J. (2003) 'Editorial: Conflict', *Gestalt Review*, 7 (3): 175–179.

Merleau-Ponty, M. (1962) *Phenomenology of Perception*. Translated from French by C. Smith. London: Routledge & Kegan Paul Ltd.

Miller, H. (1957) *Big Sur and the Oranges of Hieronymus Bosch*. New York: New Directions.

Miller, M. (1994) 'Elegiac Reflections on Isadore From', *British Gestalt Journal*, 3 (2): 76–79.

Miller, M. (2003) 'Reflections on Cornell: The Aesthetics of Sexual Love', *British Gestalt Journal*, 12 (2): 111–115.

Naranjo, C. (1982) 'Gestalt Conference Talk 1981', *The Gestalt Journal* V (1): 3–20.

Nevis, E. (1987) *Organizational Consulting: A Gestalt Approach*. New York: Gardner.

Nin, A (1990) *The Dela of Venus*. London: Penguin Books.

Ogden, T. (1982) *Projective Identification and Psychotherapeautic Technique*. London: Jason Aronson.

O'Shea, L. (2000) 'Sexuality: Old Struggles and New Challenges', *Gestalt Review* 4 (1): 8–25.

O'Shea, L. (2003) 'Reflection on Cornell: The Erotic Field', *British Gestalt Journal* 12 (2): 105–110.

Parlett, M. (1991) 'Reflections on Field Theory', *British Gestalt Journal*, 1 (2): 69–81.

Parlett, M. (1997) 'The Unified Field in Practice', *Gestalt Review*, 1 (1): 16–33.

Parlett, M. (2000) 'Creative Adjustment and the Global Field', *British Gestalt Journal*, 9 (1): 15–27.

Parlett, M. (2007) 'The Five Abilities' Summary, unpublished manuscript.

Perls, F. (1947) *Ego, Hunger and Aggression*. London: George Allen and Unwin Ltd.

Perls, F. (1948) 'Theory and Technique of Personality Integration', *American Journal of Psychotherapy*, 2: 565–586.

Perls, F., Hefferline, R. and Goodman, P. (1951) *Gestalt Therapy: Excitement and Growth in the Human Personality*. London: Souvenir Press.

Perls, F. (1969) *Gestalt Therapy Verbatim*. Moab, UT: Real People Press.

Perls, F. (1973) *The Gestalt Approach and Eye Witness to Therapy*. California: Science and Behaviour Books.

Perls, F. (1992) *Gestalt Therapy Verbatim*. Highland, NY: Gestalt Journal Press.

Perls, L. (1973) 'Some aspects of gestalt therapy'. Manuscript presented at Annual Meeting of the Orthopsychiatric Association quoted in Yontef (1993). New York: Gestalt Journal Press.

Perls, L. (1978) 'Concepts and Misconceptions of Gestalt Therapy', *Voices*, 14 (3): 31–36.

Perls, L. (1989) 'Every Novel is a Case History', *The Gestalt Journal*, XII (2): 5–10.

Perls, L. (1992) *Living at the Boundary*. Highland: Gestalt Journal Press.

Philippson, P. (2001) *Self in Relation*. Highland, NY: Gestalt Journal Press.

Philippson, P. (2002) 'A Gestalt Approach to Transference' *British Gestalt Journal*, 11 (1): 16–20.

Philippson, P. (2009) *The Emergent Self: An Existential-Gestalt Approach*. London: Karnac Books Ltd.

Polster, E. and Polster, M. (1973) *Gestalt Therapy Integrated: Contours of Theory and Practice*. New York: Vintage Books.

Polster, E. (1987) *Every Person's Life is Worth a Novel*. New York: Norton.

Polster E. (1993) 'Individuality and Communality', *British Gestalt Journal*, 2 (1): 41–43.

Polster, E. (1995) *A Population of Selves – A Therapeutic Exploration of Personal Diversity*. San Francisco: Jossey-Bass.

Resnick, R. (1995) 'Gestalt Therapy: Principles, Prisms and Perspectives: Interviewed by Malcolm Parlett', *British Gestalt Journal*, 4 (1): 3–13.

Sapriel, L. (1998) 'Can Gestalt Therapy, Self-Psychology and Inter-Subjectivity Theory be Integrated?' *British Gestalt Journal*, 7 (1): 33–44.

Sartre, J-P. (1948) *Being and Nothingness*. Translated by Barnes, H. E. New York: Philosophical Library.

Schore, A. (2003) *Affect Regulation and the Repair of the Self*. New York: Norton.

Smuts, J. (1926) *Holism and Evolution*. New York: MacMillan.

Spagnuolo-Lobb, M. (2002) 'A Gestalt Model for Addressing Psychosis', *British Gestalt Journal*, 11 (1): 5–15.

Spinelli, E. (1989) *The Interpreted World: An Introduction to Phenomenological Psychology*. London: Sage.

Staemmler, F-M. (1993) 'Projective Identification in Gestalt Therapy with Severely Impaired Clients', *British Gestalt Journal*, 2 (2): 104–110.

Staemmler, F-M. (1997) 'Cultivated Uncertainty: An Attitude for Gestalt Therapists', *British Gestalt Journal*, 6 (1): 30–40.

Staemmler, F-M. (2006) 'A Babylonian Confusion?: On the Uses and Meanings of the Term "Field" ', *British Gestalt Journal*, 15 (2): 64–83.

Staemmler, F-M. (2009) *Aggression, Time and Understanding*. Cambridge, MA: Gestalt Press.

Stern, D. (1998) *The Interpersonal World of the Infant*. New York: Karnac.

Stern, D. (2003) 'On the Other Side of the Moon: The Import of Implicit Knowledge for Gestalt Therapy' in M. Spagnuolo-Lobb, Amendt-Lyon (eds), *Creative License: The Art of Gestalt Therapy*, New York: Springer-Verlag Wien.

Trub, H. (1952) 'Healing through Meeting', in Friedman, M. (ed.) *The*

Worlds of Existentialism: A Critical Reader. Chicago: University of Chicago Press.

Van de Riet, V. Korb, M. and Gorrell, J. (1980) *Gestalt Therapy: An Introduction*, New York: Pergamon Press.

Van de Riet, V. (2001) 'Gestalt Therapy and the Phenomenological Method', *Gestalt Review*, 5 (3): 184–194.

Wertheimer, M. (1925) 'Gestalt Theory' in Ellis, W. D. (ed.), *A Source Book of Gestalt Psychology*, (1938). London: Routledge and Kegan Paul.

Wertheimer, M. (1959) *Productive Thinking*, 2nd edition, first published 1945. New York: Harper and Row.

Wheeler, G. (1991) *Gestalt Reconsidered – A New Approach to Contact and Resistance*. New York: Gardner Press.

Wheeler, G. (2000) *Beyond Individualism: Towards a New Understanding of Self, Relationship & Experience*. Hillsdale, NJ: The Analytic Press.

Williams, L. (2006) 'Spirituality and Gestalt: A Gestalt–Transpersonal Perspective', *Gestalt Review*, 10 (1): 6–21.

Wolfert, R. (2000) 'Self in Experience, Gestalt Therapy, Science and Buddhism', *British Gestalt Journal*, 9 (2): 77–86.

Wollants, G. (2008) *Gestalt Therapy: Therapy of the Situation*. Zutphen, Netherlands: Koninklijke Wohrman.

Yontef, G. (1975) 'A Review of the Practice of Gestalt Therapy' in Stephenson, F. (ed.), *Gestalt Therapy Primer: Introductory Readings in Gestalt Therapy*. Springfield, IL: Charles C. Thomas.

Yontef, G. (1981) 'The Future of Gestalt Therapy: A Symposium with G. Yontef, J. Zinker, E. Polster and L. Perls', *The Gestalt Journal*, IV (1): 3–18.

Yontef, G. (1988) 'Assimilating Diagnostic and Psychoanalytic Perspectives into Gestalt Therapy', *The Gestalt Journal*, 11 (1): 5–32.

Yontef, G. (1993) *Awareness, Dialogue & Process: Essays on Gestalt Therapy*. New York: Gestalt Journal Press.

Yontef, G. (1999) 'Awareness, Dialogue and Process: Preface to the 1998 German Edition', *The Gestalt Journal*, XXII (1): 9–20.

Yontef, G. (2002) 'The Relational Attitude in Gestalt Theory & Practice,' *International Gestalt Journal*, 25 (1): 15–36.

Yontef, G. (1996) 'Supervision from a Gestalt Therapy Perspective', *British Gestalt Journal*, 5 (2) 92–102.

Zinker J. (1977) *Creative Process in Gestalt Therapy*. New York: Vintage Books.